Walks For All Ages
Snowdonia &
North West Wales

WALKS FOR ALL AGES

SNOWDONIA & NORTH WEST WALES

HUGH TAYLOR & MOIRA McCROSSAN

BRADWELL
BOOKS

Published by Bradwell Books
9 Orgreave Close Sheffield S13 9NP
Email: books@bradwellbooks.co.uk

British Library Cataloguing in Publication Data: a catalogue record for this book is available from the British Library.

1st Edition

ISBN: 9781909914353

Print: Gomer Press, Llandysul, Ceredigion SA44 4JL

Design by: Erik Siewko Creative, Derbyshire.
eriksiewko@gmail.com

Photograph Credits: © Hugh Taylor & Moira McCrossan
and credited separately where applicable.

Maps: Contain Ordnance Survey data
© Crown copyright and database right 2015

Ordnance Survey licence number 100039353

The information in this book has been produced in good faith and is intended as a general guide. Bradwell Books and its authors have made all reasonable efforts to ensure that the details are correct at the time of publication. Bradwell Books and the author cannot accept any responsibility for any changes that have taken place subsequent to the book being published. It is the responsibility of individuals undertaking any of the walks listed in this publication to exercise due care and consideration for the health and wellbeing of each other in the party. Particular care should be taken if you are inexperienced. The walks in this book are not especially strenuous but individuals taking part should ensure they are fit and able to complete the walk before setting off.

INTRODUCTION

THIS ANCIENT AND HISTORIC PART OF BRITAIN IS A PLACE OF GREAT BEAUTY AND LEGEND. FROM ITS OUTSTANDING COASTLINE TO THE COUNTRY'S HIGHEST MOUNTAIN IT IS STEEPED IN STORY AND LEGEND. IT WAS ALSO ONCE A HIGHLY INDUSTRIALISED SOCIETY AND MANY OF THE WALKS WE HAVE CHOSEN FOR THIS BOOK WILL BRING THE STORY OF THESE INDUSTRIES TO LIFE.

Mining was once a mainstay of the economy and was responsible for the development of a communications infrastructure which included road and bridge building. Its mighty oak trees provided the raw materials for house and boat building, for powering the furnaces of the Industrial Revolution and for the tanning of leather.

There used to be gold in them thar hills and in the 19th century Wales had its own gold rush. It was soon over and all that remains are the ruins of the mines and ancillary buildings. Lead mines, slate and granite quarries lasted longer and as you wander through the book you will learn about the various processes involved including the process of smelting at the Hafna Mill. Throughout Britain Welsh is synonymous with slate and in the National Slate Museum you can still see it being worked, then wander through the homes of the workers to see how they lived at various times. On the coast you'll find the granite quarries that supplied cobbles for the city streets, and the small village where the workers lived which became a hippie commune after it was abandoned and is now the Welsh Language Centre.

Communications extended to the railways and many narrow-gauge rails were laid to transport the materials to and from the quarries, mines and foundries. Many have been preserved as heritage railways including the world-famous Ffestiniog Railway, and you'll also encounter the Llanberis Lake Railway and the Snowdon Mountain Railway, on which you can ride all the way to the summit.

Wandering through the history of the land you will encounter people here like the Welsh Wizard, David Lloyd George, Prime Minister of Great Britain, and young Mary Jones, whose simple, but deeply held faith led her on a 25-mile barefoot walk to buy a bible and indirectly led to the foundation of The British and Foreign Bibles Society.

Almost legendary is the mysterious 6th-century Bard, Taliesin, one of the first recorded poets in the Welsh language, who also crops up in Arthurian Legend as the son of Merlin. Arthur himself features in this book at the Bearded Lake, where he slew a fearsome monster after an epic struggle. Back on the coast you can pick up the trail of the most Parisian of all fictional detectives, Inspector Maigret, while the Rupert Bear connection and the tale of Prince Lllywelyn's fearless hound, Gelert, will delight children.

BETWS-Y-COED

A LOVELY WOODLAND AND RIVER WALK WITH TWO MAJOR
ATTRACTIONS TO VISIT AFTERWARDS.

Betws-y-Coed translates as the 'prayer house in the wood' and the name comes from the Church of St Michael, which was built on the banks of the River Conwy in the 14th century, although a monastery existed here as far back as the 6th century. It's the oldest building in the town and although not part of the walk is well worth a visit. By the late 20th century it was in a poor state of repair and a group was formed to preserve it and they now hold a lease on the building. It's open most days, from Easter until the end of October, and at other times the key is available from the Conwy Valley Railway Museum.

This walk goes through woodland and follows the course of the Afon Llugwy as far as the old Miners' Bridge where the lead miners crossed the river on their way to work. It's a rather unusual and very steep bridge, almost like a ladder. Lead mining was the mainstay of this and other parts of North West Wales and heralded the development of a communications infrastructure. The construction of the Telford Bridge over the Conwy brought more coach based transport through the village and it soon became a major coaching hub. The bridge is worth visiting after the walk. One of the arches has an inscription stating that it was built in the year of the Battle of Waterloo, 1815, which explains why it is called the Waterloo Bridge.

Behind the railway station you will find the excellent Conwy Valley Railway Museum and Model Shop. Children will love the miniature railway, which takes a ten-minute trip round the museum grounds. During the tourist season trains run every day. It is mostly pulled by a diesel locomotive but at weekends they use steam.

There's also the unique electric tramcar with a 15-inch gauge running along half a mile of track. For children there are dodgem cars, one of which is Postman Pat's van, and many model railway layouts as well as the Model Shop, crammed full of toys for children of all ages. There are Airfix kits, Hornby trains sets and much more. The authors and the publishers accept no responsibility for your actions should you enter this part of the museum.

THE BASICS

Distance: 2¼ miles / 3.75km

Gradient: A couple of minor gradients, one short, steep section. The return leg is downhill all the way

Severity: Moderate

Approx. time to walk: 1 - 1¼ hours

Stiles: None

Maps: OS Explorer OL17 (Snowdon, Conway Valley)

Path description: Pavement, footpaths and forest road

Start Point: From the car park at Betws-y-Coed station (GR SH 794565)

Parking: Free parking at Betws-y-Coed Station (LL24 0AE)

Dog friendly: Yes, one short section where they must be kept on leads. This is signed

Public toilets: At the car park and on the route

Nearest food: Spinnaker café opposite the car park

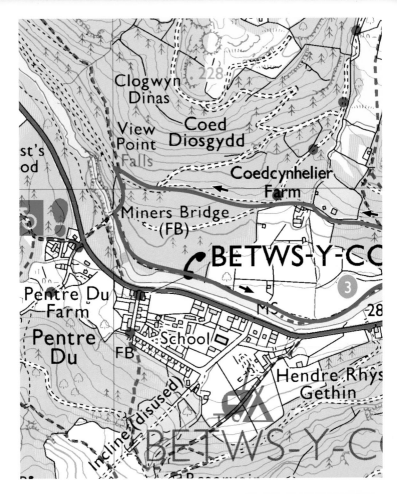

1. Facing the railway station turn left then left again onto a path that runs past the information centre for Snowdonia National Park and then goes through a car park to emerge onto the road opposite the Royal Oak Hotel. Turn right here and walk along the street to reach a junction on the right signed for Trefriw. Cross this bridge then turn left to arrive at another car park with toilets.

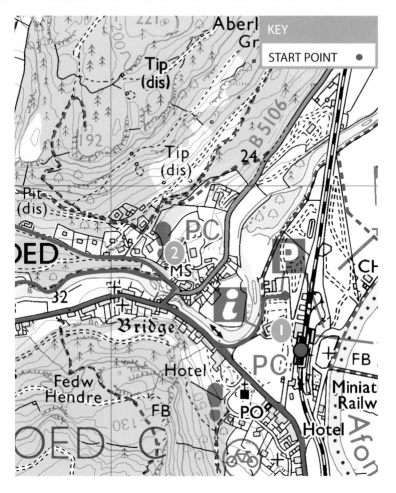

2. Veer left to go through a picnic area by the riverside then ahead onto a wooden walkway into the woods. Look out for illustrations of various beasties attached to the trees on this section. When this ends continue on the footpath until it divides. Keep left following the path by the riverside.

3. Soon after this you will pass another picnic area and then a rocky outcrop with an interesting little cave. Go through a kissing gate here and follow a well-defined footpath that soon turns left to follow the edge of the river. Signs indicate that this is a section where you must keep your dog on a lead. After crossing a footbridge the path turns right to go past some old oak trees and eventually rises through the wood to reach another kissing gate. After you have gone through this the path gets

rougher and you will need to take care as the rocks and exposed tree roots can be slippery when wet. Eventually the path will climb slightly to reach the unusual miners' bridge.

4. Turn right here and follow a line indicated by wooden posts uphill. This is a rather steep section but it is mercifully short. Just slow down and take it easy. When the path skirts round an uprooted tree base it continues uphill to the left and then reaches a junction with a forest road. Just across this and on the path that continues uphill is a bench seat where you can get your breath back.

5. Turn right onto the forest road and head along it and then downhill. This becomes a tarmac lane then ends at the car park by the river and the picnic area. Retrace your steps from here back through the town to the car park. The visitor centre is worth exploring and Betws-y-Coed has several shops you may want to go into. The children will make a beeline for the Bubble Shop at the Information Centre.

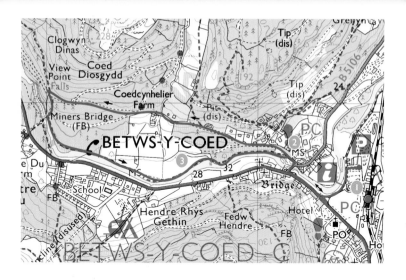

LLYN GEIRIONYDD

A GENTLE STROLL ROUND LLYN GEIRIONYDD TO THE BIRTHPLACE OF TALIESIN, THE GREAT WELSH BARD OF THE 6TH CENTURY.

Taliesin was one of the first recorded poets of the Welsh language. He was reputedly born here and the walk takes you to an unusual monument, a boulder, with a stone pillar and wooden cross, commemorating him. This was erected in 1850 by Lord Willougby de Eresby of Gwydir Castle. Unsurprisingly not a lot is actually known about Taliesin's life other than from a brief mention in an ancient Saxon manuscript. The Book of Taliesin contains several of his poems including one that praises King Urien of Rheged and mentions the Eden Valley in Cumbria. Others honour Cynan Garwyn, a King of Powys. The poet Gwilym Cowlyd, who thought that the Eisteddfod had become too anglicised, chose this spot to hold an alternative festival in 1863. The Arwest Glan Geirionydd, as it was called, continued to be held here every year until 1927.

Of course, with little in the way of actual documentation Taliesin became the subject of legend. He crops up in Arthurian Legend as the son of Merlin. He supposedly had magical powers, could change his shape at will and was the finest musician and poet of his generation. The Victorian poet Tennyson included him in his poem cycle The Idylls of the King, making him the court jester and minstrel.

The very narrow roads that lead to this remote lake mean that it is not easy to get to the start of this walk. But it is more than worth the effort. The landscape here is idyllic but it was not always so.

The car park at the start was once a massive spoil heap for the nearby Pandora Mine, and before the conifer woodlands were planted this would have been open land scarred by the industrial process. The mine opened in 1868 and although not worked continuously was still being used to extract lead and zinc as late as 1931.

Previously part of the Forestry Commission the area is now under the control of Natural Resources Wales. It's a very popular spot in summer as it is the only lake in Wales where people can use power boats or go water skiing. There's no point in taking a fishing rod, though. Waste from the mining process put paid to any fish in the lake a long time ago.

THE BASICS

Distance: 2 miles /3.2km

Gradient: Mostly flat

Severity: Easy

Approx. time to walk: 1 - 1½ hours

Stiles: Two

Map: OS Explorer OL17 (Snowdon, Conwy Valley)

Path description: Surfaced lane, forest road, footpaths

Start point: Forestry Commission Wales car park at Llyn Geirionydd (GR SH 763604)

Parking: Forestry Commission Wales Car Park at Llyn Geirionydd (free). Nearest postcode (LL27 0YZ)

Dog friendly: Yes, if the dog can get through the stiles

Public toilets: In the car park but open in the summer months only

Nearest food: Betws-y-Coed. This is a favourite picnic spot with several picnic tables so why not bring your own?

LLYN GEIRIONYDD WALK

1. Leave the car park and turn left. Head along the narrow lane to pass the end of the lake then turn right. Pass by a traffic gate and walk along a forest road that runs past the lake. When this road bends left, veer right onto a footpath then shortly afterwards cross a stile.

2. Walk along a footpath by the side of the lake then enter woodland. You are never far from the water's edge on this path and recent tree felling means that you will have some grand views. When you reach the end of the forest path, cross over another stile and keep ahead on a footpath that runs beside a dry stone wall.

3. When you come to a fork in the path the way-marker indicates a turn to the right. But keep ahead here on a broad grassy path that heads gently uphill to reach the monument to Taliesin. From the monument head back the way you came then turn left onto a track and follow it past an old stone building on your right then across the top of the lake to exit via a kissing gate onto a lane.

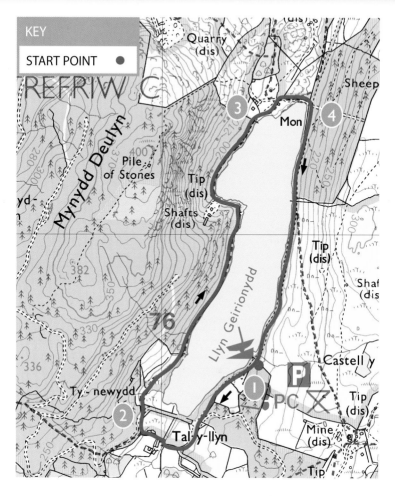

KEY

START POINT ●

4. Turn right here and follow this, passing through two gates to return to the car park.

TREFRIW

AN EXCITING TRAIL THROUGH A FOREST PARK ROUND THE
REMAINS OF A ONCE THRIVING MINING INDUSTRY.

Travel back a century or so and you would find this area to be a hive of activity, where most of the inhabitants were involved in the industry. However, as none of mines were greatly profitable and work could be sporadic, the miners also undertook seasonal work on local farms or maintained their own small farms to eke out an existence.

Young boys would start at the Parc Mine by loading the processed ore onto ladders. Their ambition was always to get a job underground because of the higher pay. They would start off as a 'tea boy' collecting and refilling the miners' flasks. Then they would graduate to clearing the debris from the rails after the rock was blasted, hoping eventually to become a timber man, responsible for installing the props, or even a driller.

The Hafna Mill, where the walk begins, opened in 1879 and processed lead ore from the nearby mine of the same name. The ore was delivered to the top of the mill, where it was graded and then slid down a chute to be crushed before moving on to the next stage in the process.

Water was used to wash away the waste material and the refined ore was then moved on to the smelter and finally the smelted lead was poured into moulds and stacked ready to transport. Hafna was different from the other mills in the area in that it had an integral smelter.

Parc Mine was the largest of the mines in this area and also the last working mine, continuing into the 1960s. But it was never really profitable and changed hands many times. It survived so long because it was taken over by a South African company in the mid-20th century. They invested heavily and introduced new technology. The mine and mill here kept 175 people in employment and it was only falling prices coupled with a deterioration in the amount of ore in the rock that finally forced it to close.

THE BASICS

Distance: 2¼ miles / 3.6km
Gradient: One steep descent and several long slow climbs
Severity: Severe
Approx. time to walk: 1½ – 2 hours
Stiles: Only one at the end
Map: OS Explorer OL17 (Snowdonia, Conwy Valley)
Path description: Forest roads and rough footpaths. Well way-marked
Start point: Hafna car park. (GR SH 781601)
Parking: Hafna Car Park (south-west of Llanrwst). Nearest postcode (LL27 0JB)
Dog friendly: Yes. The one stile can be avoided by keeping ahead at the last turn
Public toilets: None; nearest are in Betws-y-Coed
Nearest food: None; nearest is in Betws-y-Coed

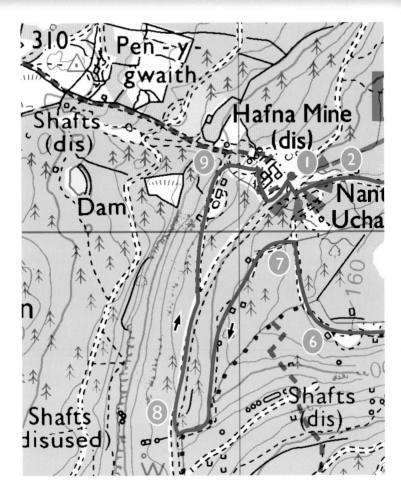

1. Start from the car park at Hafna. The final stage of the walk will take you through the old mine buildings. Head to the opposite end of the car park from the entrance, go past a gate and head uphill on a well-surfaced forest road following the red way-markers with crossed pick and hammer of the Miners' Trail. Keep on this road until you encounter the next way-marker and turn right onto a narrow footpath.

2. This is a steep, often muddy section going downhill through the wood. A walking pole and well-soled shoes or boots are required. After a short distance this levels off to become a pleasant stroll through the forest. Towards the end of this section it heads downhill again to intersect with the main road.

3. Cross the road to the next listening post on the Miners' Trail then continue on a very

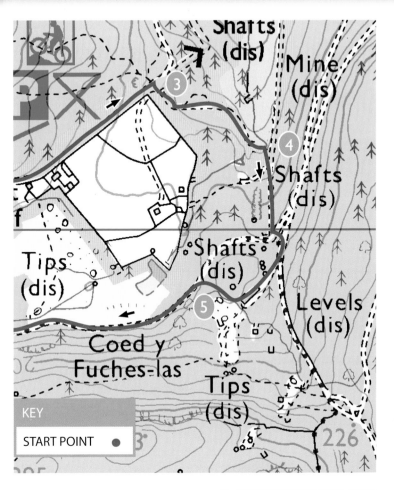

KEY

START POINT ●

pleasant woodland path. Eventually this will head uphill to reach the remains of the Parc Mine (Mwynglawdd Parc). Various signs will warn you of dangers from old mine workings. Stick to the way-marked path and don't let children wander off on their own. Mined lead and zinc was brought here and loaded into trucks that were originally hauled by ponies along a tramway to the crushing mill. Walking away from the mine interpretation board veer right from the path to explore Kneebone's Cutting then return to the path.

4. Exit the path to the cutting and turn sharp right then right again where the path reaches a junction. Now head uphill on a long slow incline, keeping ahead at the first crossroads then turning right at the next. There's a marker post there so you can't go wrong.

5. This narrow footpath takes you once again through woods to reach the ruins of the Parc Mine Office, passing a ventilation shaft then re-joining the forest road. Turn left.

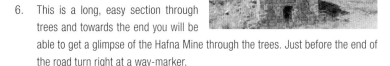

6. This is a long, easy section through trees and towards the end you will be able to get a glimpse of the Hafna Mine through the trees. Just before the end of the road turn right at a way-marker.

7. This uphill section, on a well-surfaced narrow footpath, is one of the most interesting parts of the walk and passes the remains of several buildings, the most interesting of which is the old mill. Spend time exploring this before continuing uphill on the footpath. There are two sets of steps on this steep section. Eventually the footpath will reach the road. Turn right onto it.

8. This downhill section is on a road so watch out for cars. When you reach a junction with a way-marker turn left onto a forest road. This part has the only stile so if you have a dog you may prefer to keep ahead on the road to return to the car park.

9. Head uphill once more and when the road starts to turn left, go right to cross a stile. Then descend a set of steps. This very steep section has steps all the way down. You can then explore the remains of the Hafna Mine and Mill, which was the only mine in this area with its own smelt house, built in the 1880s. From the bottom level of the mill a footpath will take you down a gentle incline back to the car park.

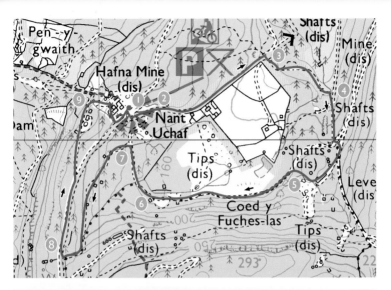

ABERGWYNGREGYN

Visit the spectacular Aber Falls on a well-surfaced footpath suitable for everyone including pushchairs. The return route is on a forest footpath. Dog walkers and pushchair pushers can return by the outward route.

This is an easy walk to one of the highest waterfalls in Wales. Its name in Welsh, Rhaeadr Fawr, means 'big waterfall'. The waters of the Afon Goch on their journey down from the Carneddau mountains finally tumble from the top of a cliff into a deep pool a hundred and twenty feet below. It is possible to dive into the pool, formed by the water hitting the rocks for centuries, but it's not recommended, as it is always freezing cold.

On the path up to the falls you will be passing an alder and ash woodland that has been coppiced for charcoal production, and on the right of the path opposite the exhibition centre you may be able to see charcoal burners. The exhibition centre was once Nant Farmhouse, which was built as a permanent dwelling, unlike many of the other habitations in this valley, which were only ever intended as summer homesteads. In the centre there is a section cut from a tree which is used to illustrate 214 years in the history of the valley. The tree itself was first planted as an acorn in 1782 by woodsmen working for the Penrhyn Estate. Nant Farmhouse was built in 1799. In the winter of 1895 the waterfall froze solid. Electricity first arrived in 1939. The Forestry Commission were here in 1958 planting the first of the conifers and in 1978 the last red squirrel was seen.

Shortly past the exhibition centre is a wooden enclosure containing a weather recording station and further on if you study the ground carefully you may see a burial mound from the Bronze Age. All around are herds of wild horses roaming freely.

When you start to pass through a small wood of ancient ash trees look out for an interpretation board, which describes some of the lichens growing on the trunks, many of them rare.

Taking a field guide to lichens on this walk will keep children amused while they see how many different types they can spot and identify. The woodland is also very rich in insect life and supports a number of woodland and upland birds. Another field guide will help to identify those you spot.

THE BASICS

Distance: 2½ miles / 4km

Gradient: One short, steep section leading up to the forest path for the return

Severity: Moderate

Approx. time to walk: 2 hours

Stiles: Two on the return route but they can be avoided by returning via the path

Map: OS Explorer OL17 (Snowdon, Conwy Valley)

Path description: A very well-surfaced, broad footpath to the falls. Return via rough footpath through woodland

Start point: Bont Newydd car park. (GR SH 662720)

Parking: At Bont Newydd (pay and display), nearest postcode (LL33 0LP)

Dog friendly: Yes. If the dog can't manage the stiles simply return by the outward route

Public toilets: At the upper car park

Nearest food: Café and information centre at the Hen Felin

1. From the car park go through a gate onto the riverside path and go along it. There is one section where the path heads uphill on stone steps. Then it descends to cross a bridge. It's worth stopping for a moment here to look at the river. Continue on the footpath from the bridge to go through an iron gate and then turn right into Coedydd Aber Nature Reserve.

2. A broad well-surfaced footpath leads from here all the way to the falls. When it meets a path junction by a wooden shelter and an interpretation board keep right. The path climbs then levels off a bit. There are superb views of the surrounding countryside and several benches where you can stop for a rest or just to enjoy your surroundings. When you reach a junction with a narrow footpath heading left into the trees keep straight ahead.

3. A sign here will tell you that it is half an hour to the falls on either path. Keep on the main footpath. You'll pass the stump of a sawn alder tree with an interpretation board explaining why it was cut, how old it was and what the wood has been used for. Shortly after this you will reach the visitor centre where a display board will map out a time line of significant events linked to the rings on another piece of sawn tree.

4. From here continue along the path passing a weather station then going through a gate to enter an area where an upland hay meadow is being restored. It's particularly important to close the gates to avoid stock getting in and eating the grass. In another short while you will exit the project through another gate. Look out for another tree stump and an interpretation board explaining about lichens. If you have children with you, see how many different types of lichen they can spot.

5. Eventually the path will come to a set of steps leading uphill to a view point over the falls. If you prefer you can continue on the path to reach this viewpoint, which is much less of a climb. Then the path continues all the way to the foot of the falls after passing

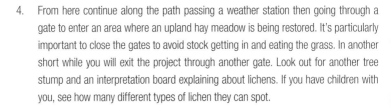

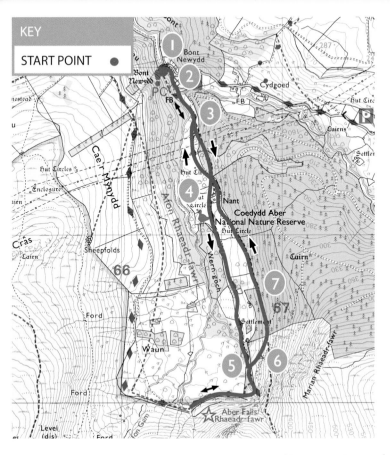

through a metal gate. Once you have spent some time at the falls return to this gate and just before it veer right across the grass to cross a stile.

6. This leads into National Trust land and passes through a boulder field. Veer right here and follow the narrow path uphill, taking care crossing the boulders, then cross another stile and enter the woods.

7. From here a narrow footpath goes through the woods, contouring the hill. It is more or less flat except for some downhill sections. Eventually it will come to a kissing gate. Go through this and continue to a path by the edge of the wood. Then it re-enters the woods and heads downhill to re-join the broad path you walked along earlier. Turn right here and retrace your steps back to the car park.

MOELFRE

This walk has it all. Lovely countryside, meadows, woodland and quiet country lanes; then a walk through several millennia of Welsh history from the Neolithic to the 6th century; followed by a very popular family beach; then a coastal path walking through three aeons of geological formation; and finally tales of shipwrecks and heroic rescues.

The first point of interest you will reach is the Lligwy Burial Chamber. This Neolithic burial chamber was created sometime prior to 3000 BCE. The skills and ingenuity of the small farming community are evident in the giant capstone, which weighs around 25 tons. How did they manage to move it with neither wheels nor metal tools? When archaeologists excavated this site in 1908–9 they uncovered the bones of around thirty men, women and children.

A bit further on you will visit Din Lligwy, a Romano-British village of mainly stone buildings within a defensive wall. It would have been built in the latter part of the Roman occupation of Wales. The distinctive round and rectangular huts were built over a period as the village expanded and developed. The main

period of occupation was probably during the 4th century. When the site was excavated in the early years of the 20th century, 3rd-century pot shards of Roman origin were found, as well as tools fashioned from animal bones and even a musical instrument. Iron working and possibly even smelting would have been the main economic activity here. Certainly the excavation of one of the workshops revealed lots of iron slag, charcoal and oak, which would suggest smelting. The settlement may well pre-date the Romans, though, and may even have existed as far back as the Iron Age.

Look out for the ruin of the medieval chapel, which you will see on your way back to the road from the village. It would have been the religious centre for the scattered agrarian community that lived here at that time.

Towards the end of the coastal section of this walk you will come across the monument to the 19th-century clipper the Royal Charter, which was wrecked nearby on 26 October 1859. A force 12 hurricane drove it onto a sandbank and then onto the rocks with few survivors. Around 450 people lost their lives. Exactly a century later Moelfre lifeboat crew rescued everyone on board the Hindlea, when it too got into difficulties here.

THE BASICS

Distance: 5 miles / 8km

Gradient: Mostly flat but a few undulations on the coastal path

Severity: Easy

Approx. time to walk: 3 hours at least. Makes a great family day outing with time spent on the beach

Stiles: None on the walk (one if you visit the Royal Charter Memorial)

Map: OS Explorer 263 (Anglesey East)

Path description: Country lanes, field footpaths and coastal path

Start point: Car park in Moelfre (GR SH 511862)

Parking: Free car parking in Moelfre (LL72 8LT)

Dog friendly: A few sections where you need to keep dog on a short lead. Signed

Public toilets: At the car park

Nearest food: Ann's Pantry near Porth Moelfre and a café halfway round on Lligwy Bay at the beach car park

MOELFRE

1. Leave the car park by the pedestrian exit next to the toilet block and turn left. Walk along the pavement, heading uphill to reach a junction in front of the library. Turn left here then veer right across a car parking area and along a lane.

2. Continue on this, passing a metal gate on the right and then the house at Tyn Coed on your left. Keep to the surfaced lane and ignore the footpath heading off to the left. When that ends at a cottage, keep left towards a metal gate then turn left at a way-marker onto the Gallgo Circular Walk.

3. Keep ahead on this footpath to go through a kissing gate and across a field. The path follows the line of a hedge then when that ends the path curves to the right to reach another gate in the far hedge. Go through this and head diagonally left to reach another kissing gate in the corner of the field. Go through this and along an overgrown section of path at the edge of woodland then through another kissing gate and turn left along the edge of a field. This leads to a last kissing gate on this section. Go through it and turn right onto a lane.

4. You are now on the most interesting section of this walk. Keep on this lane until you arrive at a kissing gate on your left at a sign for the Lligwy Burial Chamber. Go through and then enter the fenced area of the chamber to explore the monument which was built around 2500–2000 BCE. When you have seen enough return to the road and turn left.

5. Keep on the lane until it widens just before a right turn and cross over to a kissing gate and interpretation board. Go through the gate and down a set of stone steps. Then follow the path along the edge of the field. Turn left at a sign pointing to Din Lligwy. Follow the well-trodden path towards a kissing gate in a wall. Go through it and the next gate then enter woodland and ascend some stone steps to the entrance path to the settlement, which is ringed by trees. When you have seen it all return to the first kissing gate and keep ahead to arrive at the remains of a mediaeval chapel. From there return to the road and keep left.

6. The lane runs downhill. Keep ahead at crossroads then straight on to arrive at the beach. Just after the café in the car park turn right onto the coastal path and follow it back to the village.

7. Just after the Royal Charter Monument the path enters a caravan site. Turn right here and follow the track through the site. When it reaches a barrier go through it and turn left at a footpath sign. Follow the way-markers to turn right then left onto a narrow footpath between hedges, emerging through a kissing gate and turning right to follow the edge of a meadow. Then turn left along another meadow hedge, through a tight kissing gate in the corner, along another stretch of path and through a wooden gate and beyond it one last kissing gate. Turn left then right at a track and finally emerge on a road. Keep ahead on this through the village to arrive at the beach, then pass the hotel and Ann's Pantry to arrive at a junction where you turn right to get back to the car park.

LLANDDWYN IN WELSH MEANS THE CHURCH OF ST
DWYNWEN AND WAS THE HOME OF THE WOMAN KNOWN AS
THE WELSH VALENTINE, THE PATRON SAINT OF LOVERS, WHOSE
FEAST DAY IS 25 JANUARY.

Dwynwen was one of 24 daughters of King Brychan of Brycheiniog, who lived in the 5th century. On one occasion the King of Gwynedd and one of his sons, Prince Maelon, visited the court. Maelon fell in love with Dwynwen and asked her to marry him. Although she had refused, he asked her father for her hand the very next morning. The king asked his daughter if she loved him and she replied that she did not. So Maelon and his father were told to leave the next day. That night Maelon visited Dwywen in her bedchamber and forced himself upon her. She was scared to tell her father what had happened for she feared there would be a war, so she left the castle and wandered in the wood, sat down and fell asleep.

She dreamed of an angel who asked her why she was so sad. She told her tale and said she wished Maelon were dead. On her return to the castle she found that Maelon had been turned into a block of ice. She was distraught. That night the angel returned and she begged him to release Maelon. He said that he would grant her three wishes. Her first was that Maelon should be released and live a good and honest life. The second was that God would watch over all true lovers; and the last that in penance for her vanity she should never marry. They were all granted. Maelon was released, married and raised a family. Dwynwen left her father's home and moved to Llanddwyn Island, where she built a small chapel to live in.

People would visit her there asking her to pray for their souls and young women would come to ask her if the love they had found was true. She sent them to her well with instructions to throw bread on the water and cover it with their lover's handkerchief. If the love was true the surface of the water would not even ripple. If, however, it was false a huge angry eel would surface and devour the bread. Dwynwen died in 465 and is believed to be buried in her chapel.

THE BASICS

Distance: 4 miles / 6km

Gradient: Fairly flat. Some easy and short gradients on the island

Severity: Easy

Approx. time to walk: 2 - 2½ hours

Stiles: None

Map: OS Explorer 263 (Anglesey East)

Path description: Well-surfaced footpaths, sandy beach

Start point: Beach Car Park at Llanddwyn Bay (GR SH 405635)

Parking: Beach Car Park at Llanddwyn Bay (payment in pound coins is needed to get through barrier to access this part of Anglesey) (LL61 6SG Newborough)

Dog friendly: Not very. Dogs are barred from the island and a large part of the beach from 1 May to 30 September

Public toilets: At car park

Nearest food: Mobile snack and ice cream bars in the car park in the summer. Otherwise the nearest is in Newborough

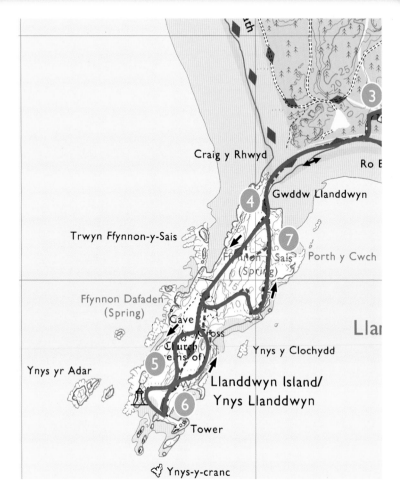

Craig y Rhwyd

Ro B

Gwddw Llanddwyn

Trwyn Ffynnon-y-Sais

Ffynnon Sais
(Spring)

Porth y Cwch

Ffynnon Dafaden
(Spring)

Cave
Cross

Church
...ins of

Ynys y Clochydd

Ynys yr Adar

Llanddwyn Island/
Ynys Llanddwyn

Ll

Tower

Ynys-y-cranc

1.   Leave the car park on a path leading away from the right-hand side of the toilet block. In 150 metres this will arrive at a central information area with a series of carved wooden sculptures designed by the pupils of Newborough School in 2013. From the information area go onto a wooden boardwalk and follow it to reach a junction with a well-surfaced road through the forest. Turn left.

2.   In a short distance a footpath starts to the right of this road. Continue along that, stopping occasionally to look at the flip-up information posts for children. When you reach a junction where the green way-markers point right, keep straight ahead. There is a set of parallel bars here on a sandy surface and a bench seat. Soon the path ends and you are back on the forest road. When this reaches a

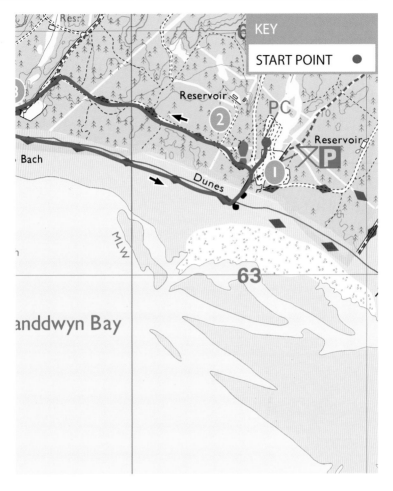

junction turn left and keep on to reach a turning area by the beach.

3. Turn right here onto a sandy footpath going along the edge of a wood and by the beach. When this finally reaches the beach walk across it to the north-east end of the island. Look out for the pillows of rock on the beach here, created by lava erupting onto the ocean floor with each successive layer piling on top of the one below. Further movement in the earth's crust tilted the pillows on their side. When you reach a set of stone steps climbing up onto the island you will note the green and red fragments in the rocks, caused by the icy sea water shattering the red-hot lava.

4. At the top of the steps follow a narrow footpath across the island to go through a gate by a cattle grid. The almost vertical rocks here were formed from the fine muds of the ocean floor. Further on, in the rocks with bands of green and red, the red is jasper, a semi-precious stone. Continue along the path to reach the large stone cross, commemorating St Dwynwen. Beyond it the path continues to an old lighthouse, built in 1845 to the same design as an Anglesey windmill. There's an older beacon to the left of this, which now operates as an automated warning light.

5. Follow the path round past the smaller of the lighthouses to Porth Twr beach. The multi-coloured rocks here, caused by movement of the ocean plates, were described as the 'mélange' by the geologist Edward Greenly.

6. From here pass by the cottages that were built to house the pilots who guided boats through the Menai Strait. The lifeboat station closed in 1903 but the cannon used to summons the crew sits in front of the cottages. Following the path round from the cottages you will come to the ruin of St Dwynwen's Chapel and just across the path from it another Celtic Cross with the inscription 'They lie around did living tread, this sacred ground now silent – dead.' Not far along the path from here is a stile on the right. Cross this to go to a ruined stone structure that is reputedly all that remains of the saint's well. From here continue along the path to reach the beach.

7. From here retrace your steps to the car park. However, if the tide is well out, turn right along the beach until you come to the wooden boardwalk. Then turn left and head along a sandy path through trees to reach the forest road. Turn right along it to return to the car park.

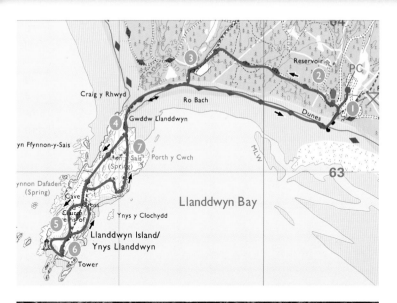

CEMAES

If you have seen the 2006 Demi Moore film, Half Light, Llanbadrig may look familiar. That's because it was used for location shots even though the story was set in Scotland.

Eglwys Llanbadrig translated from the Welsh means the church of St Patrick and the church, which you will visit, was allegedly founded by Patrick himself around AD 440 after he had been shipwrecked on the island of Ynys Badrig (Patrick's Isle), which also appears on maps as Middle Mouse. Pope Celestine I sent Patrick to Ireland to convert the inhabitants to Christianity. When his ship allegedly ran aground on Middle Mouse, he managed, somehow, to cross to Anglesey, where he landed in the bay now known as Porth Padrig. Apparently he discovered a freshwater well in a cave in the cliffs below the present churchyard and he founded a church on the spot as thanks to God for saving him.

Cemaes Bay is an area of outstanding natural beauty, and walking around it you would be hard put to argue. The village of Cemaes has a natural harbour and was for a long time a fishing port. Until the virtual demise of herring stocks in the mid-20th century, Camaes had a reputation for the salted herring it produced. Its pier, on which its prosperity depended, was seriously damaged by storms in 1828 and 1889 but local businessmen financed the reconstruction on both occasions. It has long attracted tourists, and if you visit here during the summer the beach will be full of families on holiday. Since Victorian times it has been popular with artists and celebrities and a frequent visitor was David Lloyd George.

The coastline here is a paradise for geologists. The rocks exposed by erosion belong to what they have named the Mona Complex and contains the oldest rocks in Wales. Almost as soon as you leave the car park you are walking along Precambrian rock, about 700 million years old. Look out for bluish-green limestone. You can also see some that have been in-filled with Miocene sediment. There's iron-stained quartzite, ironstone deposits, bright white quartzite and what the geologist Edward Greenly called 'mélange', a mixture of different rock particles set in a greenish rock. There are also blocks of the blood-red jasper, a semi-precious stone.

THE BASICS

Distance: 2 miles / 3.2km

Gradient: Gentle climbs: long and slow

Severity: Easy

Approx. time to walk: 1 - 1½ hours

Stiles: None

Map: OS Explorer 262 (Anglesey West)

Path description: Pavement, footpaths, country lane and coastal path

Start point: Car Park at the end of the promenade (GR SH 375937)

Parking: At the end of the promenade (free); go through village, turn left onto the A5025 and then next left then follow parking signs. Nearest postcode is (LL67 0ND)

Dog friendly: A good dog walk but keep on a short lead where signs request it

Public toilets: At the opposite end of the promenade in the pay car park

Nearest food: Café in pay car park and several food outlets in the town

CEMAES WALK

1. Exit the car park and immediately turn left past a National Trust sign to Penrhyn Mawr onto the West Coast Footpath. This runs along the top of the cliffs and provides a panoramic view across the bay and the town. Go up some steps, through a kissing gate then turn left at a junction and make your way to the end where there is a bench seat with an awesome view. When you have rested or seen enough walk back and continue along the path to reach another kissing gate. A set of steps leads down from here to an old, abandoned limekiln. Behind it is a disused quarry which was the largest one locally and a mainstay of what was once Cemaes lime and stone exports. To the front of the kiln is a small inlet where you can see bowl-like, rounded hollows at low tide, where the limestone was dissolved by fresh water.

2. Pass the limekiln and head up steps at the other side to go through another kissing gate. Then head across a field on a broad grassy path to go through another gate.

3. The path once more goes down and up steps as the path winds round another inlet and continues to reach a junction of paths. Keep ahead here and go down some steps onto the beach. The large white rock in front of you is a block of iron-stained quartzite known as The White Lady. When you have seen this return to the point where the path divides and turn left. Follow this narrow path along the edge of a field to reach a kissing gate. Exit through it onto a lane and turn left.

4. Not that far along this lane you will see the entrance to the church. But before visiting it turn left through a car park and exit it via a gate, then turn right. Head downhill to the far left end of a headland to reach Llanbadrig Point. On the shore near here are ironstone deposits that look like a road of rusting metal. Walk round the grassy mound at the point and look at the rocks there. Mostly they are bright white quartzite. Walking clockwise round the point you will encounter Greenly's 'mélange', This is where you are most likely to find the deposits of jasper. The path then starts to head uphill, still on a grassy path. Just before the churchyard is the

KEY

START POINT ●

location of Patrick's Cave. It lies below amongst the cliffs along with his well and it is inaccessible. The path now curves to the right along a ridge then descends to go through a metal kissing gate onto the lane. Turn left here to enter through the stone arch into the churchyard and visit the church. It was restored in 1884 by the 3rd Lord Stanley of Alderley, who was a Muslim. It was destroyed by an arson attack in 1985 but restored by money collected by the Friends of Llanbadrig.

5. From the church return to the car park via the lane, keeping right at both junctions.

GANLLWYD

DELIGHTFUL WOODS, WATERFALLS AND THE REMAINS OF
LONG-CLOSED GOLD MINES.

This walk will take you up along a magical valley created
by the rivers Gamlan and Mawddach, through what
were the parklands of the historic Dolmelynllyn Estate.
Although it's a bit of a pull up the first section you will
soon be gazing in wonder at the falls of Rhaeadr Ddu.
The woodlands here were planted centuries ago and
have been well managed since. The oak trees were
once used for the construction of houses and boats,
while charcoal was produced for the furnaces of the
Industrial Revolution and the oak bark was used in the
tanning of leather.

Gold was discovered in these hills during the 19th century, sparking a Welsh Gold Rush,
when this area became known as the New California. As you walk round the remains of
the old mines, the tumbledown crushing mill and the old powder hut, you will realise that
the miners who lived and worked in this inhospitable countryside would have had a hard
life. At one time this mine, the Cefn Coch Mine, was the fourth richest in the Dolgellau
gold belt and often worked jointly with the Berthlwyd mine, following the same lode.
Mining started in Cefn Coch in 1862 and continued with intermittent closures until it
closed for good in 1914.

The farmers who also worked this land must have put a lot of back-breaking toil into
making a living. This estate once supported seven farms. You may come across what
is left of a 'hafod' , a rough shelter in the hills, where the farming families moved with
their stock for the summer grazing before returning to the relative comfort of their main
dwelling below in the winter.

This estate once belonged to William Madocks, a landowner, Member of Parliament and
18th- and 19th-century improver. He was a founder of Porthmadog and Tremadog and
builder of Porthmadog's famous Cob. However, he was continually overstretching himself
and came close to bankruptcy. The poet Shelley was a friend and assisted him in fund
raising for the building of Porthmadog Cob. There's a slate tablet set into the rocks just
above the first footbridge you will encounter on this walk with a fragment of a poem
by Thomas Gray. Next to it are the very same words cut into the rock, apparently by
Madocks, but now very indistinct.

THE BASICS

Distance: 2¼ miles/ 3.6km

Gradient: Some fairly steep sections, particularly up to the waterfalls

Severity: Severe

Approx. time to walk: 2½ - 3 hours

Stiles: Five

Map: OS Explorer OL18 (Harlech, Porthmadog and Bala)

Path description: Woodland footpaths, tracks, forest roads

Start point: National Trust car park at Ganllwyd (GR SH 726243)

Parking: National Trust Car park (free) at Ganllwyd, on A470 four miles north of Dolgellau (LL40 2TF)

Dog friendly: Only if they can manage the stiles

Public toilets: In car park

Nearest food: Dolgellau

GANLLWYD WALK

1. Walk past the toilets and head to the end of the car park. Then follow a way-marker left and turn right through a gate. Cross the road, turn right beside the village hall then go through a gate and head uphill on a lane. When this curves right at a junction, keep ahead, still climbing up through woodland. When the path curves right again, veer left onto a narrow footpath and follow the way-marks through the trees to eventually reach a wooden footbridge over the river.

2. Cross this, go through a gate and turn right onto a footpath heading uphill beside the river. A signpost tells you this is the Coed Ganllwyd National Nature Reserve. On a wooden board is a poem in Welsh that was written in 2011 by pupils of the local primary schools to commemorate the 75th anniversary of the acquisition of the estate by the National Trust. The path climbs steeply up from here to reach the falls. This section can be slippery when wet as the path is very rocky. Boots or shoes with good soles are recommended and a walking pole would also be helpful. At the falls keep a hold of young children while viewing the spectacular double falls. Then continue on the footpath for a short while before turning left at a way-mark to walk on a footpath beside a dry stone wall. Although still climbing it is a much gentler incline. This is a very pleasant section through woodland. When you reach a ladder stile by a way-marker, ignore the marker and go right over the stile.

3. Then keep ahead to cross another stile, a step one this time. and follow the well-posted route through woodland and across a meadow to reach a wooden gate. Pass by this and head towards a cottage. As you approach it you will see a way-marker on your left. Follow it to get onto a forest track. Turn left and head along the track.

4. When this forks go right and head slightly uphill to another junction where you veer left onto a footpath next to a green way-marker. This will take you along a grassy footpath to reach a stile on your left. Cross this then veer right. At the next way-marker turn left onto a grassy track and head uphill. All around here are the ruined remains of the gold

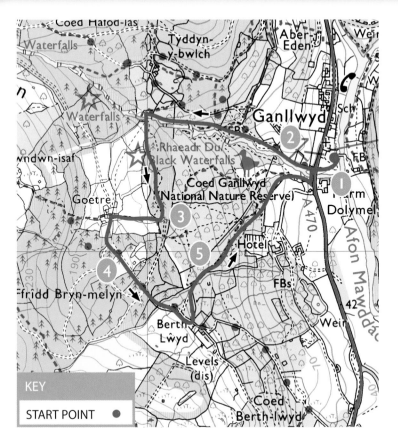

mine. The first one you pass is probably what is left of the crushing mill. Take time to explore round it but do not go inside. Then continue along the track past the next ruin, which may have been the miners' accommodation, and just as you reach what may well have been the powder shed turn left at another way-mark. Cross a ladder stile and head downhill on a grassy footpath. The view from here over the valley to the hills beyond is magnificent. Cross another ladder stile then veer towards the ruins of the cottage at Berthlwyd. From there veer left to cross yet another ladder stile, cross the track and continue downhill on a well way-marked footpath to reach a wooden bridge. Cross this, go through a gate and turn right.

5. The path now heads downhill through woodland, finally reaching a gate into a field. Cross this, go through a metal gate and turn left onto the road. Walk along this to return to the car park.

BRITHDIR

THE TORRENT WALK IS VERY POPULAR WITH DOG WALKERS AND FAMILIES, WHICH IS HARDLY SURPRISING AS THERE ARE LOTS OF INTERESTING THINGS TO ENCOUNTER AND THE WHOLE GORGE IS NOW A SITE OF SPECIAL SCIENTIFIC INTEREST (SSSI).

A few field guides on this walk will help identify the various beasties and plants you may come across, including otters and dormice and, if you are lucky, at the right time of day lesser horseshoe bats. Much easier to find and identify are the various lichens, ferns, fungi and trees. The river that runs through this walk used to be a hive of industry, providing the water and power for a fulling mill, woollen mill, iron furnace and smithy. The industry and the noise it would have produced are long gone and all you will hear is birdsong and the sounds of running water.

The path on the east side has been extensively restored by the Snowdonia National Park Authority, making it a fairly easy and safe walk although there are gradients. Originally this path was created for Baron Richards of Caerynwch House, which lies just a bit upriver from the walk. Richards used this path to extend the garden of the house, which was built in 1780. Prior to that the Richards family had occupied a much smaller 15th-century house, which can now be rented as a self-catering cottage. Caerynwch was the home of the botanist Mary Richards, who collected extensively in Africa in the second half of the 20th century. The house is still owned by the Richards family.

St Mark's Church in nearby Brithdir is in the care of the Friends of Friendless Churches. Built between 1895 and 1898 it is arguably the finest example of the Arts and Crafts style in Wales. The architect was Henry Wilson, a leading light in the movement. The doors of the church are Art Nouveau and made of oak and teak. If you are fortunate enough to be able to visit the inside you will be delighted. The colour scheme gives it a Mediterranean feel. Kids will love the intricate carvings of a hare, squirrel, rabbits, tortoise, kingfisher, dolphin and a little mouse that adorn the choir stalls. The font, pulpit and altar were all designed by Wilson. But while the Central School of Art in London made the font the architect actually made both pulpit and altar himself.

THE BASICS

Distance: 2 miles / 3.2km

Gradient: Long, slow, gentle gradients

Severity: Moderate

Approx. time to walk: 1 - 1½ hours

Stiles: None

Map: OS Explorer OL23 (Cadair Idris and Llyn Tegid)

Path description: Mainly footpaths, a short section on road

Start point: Lay-by on B4416 (GR SH 761181)

Parking: Lay-by on B4416, just off A470 east of Dolgellau (LL40 2RE)

Dog friendly: Good dog walk

Public toilets: None on the walk or nearby

Nearest food: In the village, 300 metres down the lane opposite St Mark's Church you can get sandwiches, cakes, drinks and ice creams. Dogs are welcome

BRITHDIR WALK

1. A footpath sign at the end of the lay-by indicates the start of the walk. Follow the direction arrow downhill and go through a gate. Then follow the path between two fences into woodland. From here head downhill on a clearly defined and well way-marked path through the trees. Cross a footbridge and turn left. The path continues downhill then goes round a couple of very tight turns and down some steps to arrive beside the river. Keep going along the riverside path and along a boardwalk to cross a muddy section. Eventually climb uphill on a set of steps to arrive at a lane.

2. Turn left and follow the lane downhill to a junction opposite Rose Cottage then turn left and cross a bridge.

3. At the end of the bridge turn left and go through a metal gate onto a footpath. Now head back uphill on the other side of the river. At first there are several series of steps, then a footpath. Eventually cross a footbridge and follow the path to the top of the gorge to go through a kissing gate then on up to the road.

4. Turn left here and in a few yards arrive back at the start.

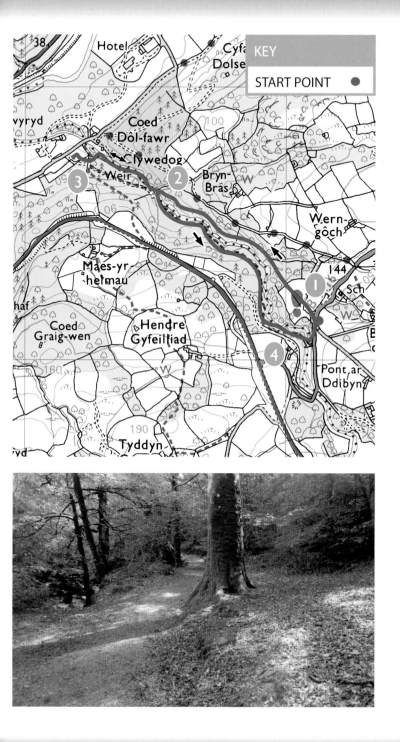

LLANFIHANGEL-Y-PENNANT

A PLEASANT AND EASY COUNTRYSIDE WALK COUPLED WITH THE STORY OF A YOUNG WELSH GIRL WHOSE THIRST FOR KNOWLEDGE LED HER ON TO A MUCH LONGER WALK.

Mary Jones was the daughter of an agricultural worker and his wife. They were Calvinistic Methodists and Mary was raised with their beliefs. She learned to read by attending the circulating Sunday schools, which were started by the leading Methodist preacher Thomas Charles. The only book available in Welsh was the Bible, and the nearest copy that Mary could access belonged to Mr and Mrs Evans, who lived in a farmhouse two miles from her home. The preacher encouraged Mary to save hard so she could buy her own copy, and that became the main ambition of her young life. It took her six years to scrape together the money by selling eggs and honey. Once she found a wallet and returned it to its owner, earning a reward of sixpence. She knew that the Revd Charles sold Welsh bibles, but he lived 25 miles away at Bala. So Mary at just 15 years old made that epic walk, barefoot, from the small cottage which you pass on this walk.

When she arrived at his home the bibles were still en route from London so Mary was sent to live with his servant for a few days until they arrived. 'When they came Mr Charles gave me three for the money, that is for the price of one. I set off home with my precious burden. I ran a great part of the way. I was so glad of my Bible.' Her unswerving devotion led the Reverend to form The British and Foreign Bibles Society, in 1804, which printed and distributed bibles throughout the world.

Mary eventually married a weaver and moved to another village. They had several children, all but one pre-deceasing her. After her husband died Mary lived on 'in a small miserable cottage'. It had an earthen floor, a couple of three-legged stools and a table with a candle on it.

She was described as wearing 'the old Welsh dress … a Jim Crow (felt hat) and a blue homespun cloak and a hood'. She carried a stick when out and, although she was blind, a lantern which she lit so others could see her. She died on 29 December 1864, just after her 80th birthday.

THE BASICS

Distance: 2½ miles / 4km
Gradient: Mostly flat
Severity: Easy
Approx. time to walk: 1½ hours
Stiles: Two
Map: OS Explorer OL23 (Cadair Idris and Llyn Tegid)
Path description: Lanes, tracks and footpaths
Start point: Car park opposite the church in Llanfihangel-y-Pennant (GR SH 672088)
Parking: Car park opposite the church in Llanfihangel-y-Pennant (LL36 9TS)
Dog friendly: Not very. The two stiles make it difficult
Public toilets: None on the route
Nearest food: In Dolgoch

1. Exit the car park in the direction of the church, then turn right onto a lane. Follow it, passing a cottage on your right, then continue to arrive at a farm just before a corner. Continue past the farm then, as the road turns right, you have arrived at the birthplace of Mary Jones.

2. When you have had a look at this go back to the corner, passing Pennant and going straight ahead through a metal gate with a sign on it for Gernos. Walk along this track, then through a gate just before the cottage at Gernos.

3. Keep left on the footpath that veers left from the track and go round the front of the cottage then continue along a grassy track. Cross a ladder stile, then a step stile over a wall and keep going until you reach a bridge on your left by a farm.

4. Turn left to cross the bridge then pass to the left of a farm building, go through a metal gate and turn right onto the farm track. When this bends left keep ahead onto a footpath and follow it in the direction indicated by the finger post along the edge of a fence.

5. When you come to a gate in the corner of the field turn left through it and keep ahead to pass to the right side of the rocky outcrop that the castle stands on. Then head across the field to cross a stile before turning left into a lane. Keep on this to arrive at the car park for castle visitors and then you can detour to visit the remains. Otherwise continue along the lane to return to the church which you can visit before returning to the car park.

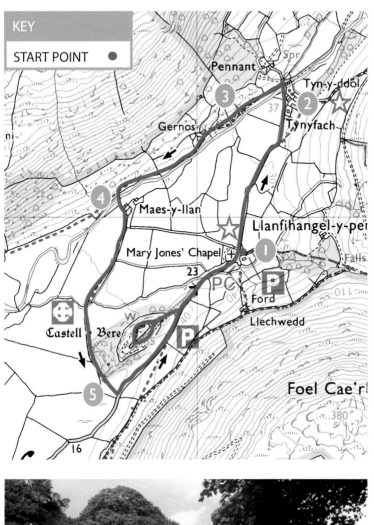

KEY

START POINT ●

TYWYN

LLYN BARFOG MEANS BEARDED LAKE. THE STORY GOES THAT IT WAS NAMED AFTER THE BEARD OF ONE OF KING ARTHUR'S KNIGHTS OF THE ROUND TABLE, OR PERHAPS IT WAS BECAUSE OF THE PROFUSION OF WATER LILIES ON ITS SURFACE.

As you head uphill you will be following in the footsteps of King Arthur towards the lair of a fearsome monster called the Afanc. It resembled a crocodile, or perhaps it was like a beaver or even a dwarf. Some say it was a demon. Walking away from the pleasant Happy Valley at the start of the walk gives no indication of how remote this lake will seem. But once past the last of the farm buildings and winding uphill on a rough and narrow track you will soon feel that sense of isolation. For the best effect do this walk on a dull and overcast day.

© John Lucas

Once you are at the water's edge and there are no other signs of life it's easy to let your imagination run riot and conjure up a vision of something dark and malevolent lurking just under the surface. According to local lore this is where the Afanc lived. Like all decent scary monsters it emerged periodically to terrorise the populace, raid the towns and villages and carry off people and livestock. People avoided the lake as anyone who got remotely close was never seen or heard of again.

Enter King Arthur, slayer of beasts and rescuer of damsels in distress. He rode uphill and right to the edge of the water. Out popped the Afanc, thinking it was lunch time, but then it was surprised when Arthur wrapped a heavy chain around it. A terrible struggle ensued, with the beast trying to get Arthur and his horse into the water and the king and steed trying to drag it onto dry land. Eventually the strength of the horse won the day and dragged the Afanc out of the lake, where Arthur slew it with his sword.

You can see the exact spot on the walk where this supposedly happened. It may be just a story but a little bit past the lake, on the walk, you will come across Carn March Arthur, the Stone of Arthur's horse, where you will easily make out the shape of Arthur's horse's hoof print deep in the rock.

© Richard Law

THE BASICS

Distance: 2¼ miles / 3.6km

Gradient: One slow gentle rise on the outward journey and a much steeper descent towards the end

Severity: Severe

Approx. time to walk: 1½ hours

Stiles: Two ladder stiles

Map: OS Explorer OL23 (Cadair Idris and Llyn Tegid)

Path description: Tracks (some rough) and footpaths

Start point: Snowdonia National Park car park in Happy Valley (GR SN 640986)

Parking: Snowdonia National Park Car Park in Happy Valley (free), on unclassified road east of Tywyn (Nearest postcode is LL36 9HY)

Dog friendly: Yes

Public toilets: None on route, nearest in Tywyn

Nearest food: Tywyn

TYWYN WALK

1. Leave the car park via a kissing gate at the far end and turn left onto a track. Follow this to reach farm buildings then turn left just before a large farmhouse, and cross a ladder stile by a gate (this can be opened for your dog). Then keep ahead on the track to cross a second ladder stile. Keep on this track uphill, keeping right at each of two junctions, then go through a gate at the top of the hill and follow the track to another junction where you keep right to pass a way-marker and arrive at another gate. Go through this and in a short distance the lake will come into view.

2. When the grassy footpath forks to go down to the lakeside, keep right and head uphill again then down the other side heading towards a way-marker. Keep right here and follow the path to reach a track then follow it, going through a gate and continuing to pass the stone at Carn March Arthur. By now you should have a splendid view across the estuary of the River Dovey and the Dyfi National Nature Reserve on your left. Go through another gate then keep going as the path turns right and goes downhill to arrive at a junction beside a cottage.

3. Turn right to go through a gate and then walk past the rear of the cottage on a grassy track, which soon heads rather steeply downhill and becomes a rough, rocky, rutted track. Take great care on this section. Eventually go through a gate near the bottom and arrive back at the outward path. Follow this back to the car park.

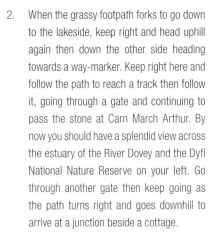

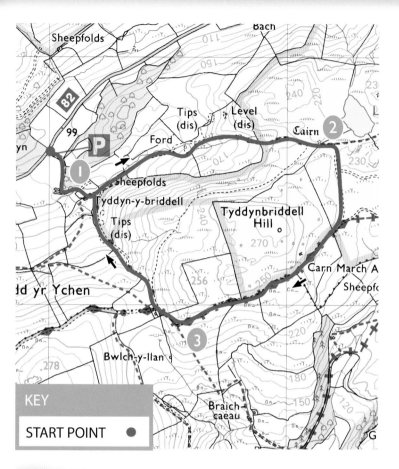

KEY

START POINT ●

LLANBERIS

This gentle stroll has a lakeside walk, country park, steam heritage railway and the National Slate Museum.

You really are spoiled for choice on this walk and it would be a good idea to spend the entire day in Llanberis. Next to the start of the walk is Electric Mountain, the visitor centre for the First Hydro Company's Dinorwic Power Station. Admission to the centre is free but there is a charge for the visit to the power station itself.

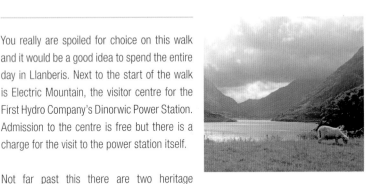

Not far past this there are two heritage railways. On the left is the station for the Llanberis Lake Railway, which you pass on the return route. A little further along on the right, but not on the walk, is the Snowdon Mountain Railway, a narrow-gauge rack and pinion railway that you can ride all the way to the summit of the highest mountain in Wales. Then there are the ruins of the 13th-century Dolbadarn Castle, which you can explore on the early part of the walk. It has a magnificent round tower and the climb up is rewarded with the wonderful views of the surrounding landscape. But the best of the attractions you will pass is the National Slate Museum.

This gem of industrial heritage is located in the former workshops of the now defunct Dinorwic Slate Quarry. Built in 1870 and finally closed in 1969, it expertly unfolds the story of slate quarrying. You'll find blacksmiths' forges, a sawmill, the largest working waterwheel in mainland Britain and even an iron foundry complete with the wooden moulds needed to cast replacement parts like wheels and axles. Various talks and demonstrations help to bring the story alive.

The narrow-gauge rails of the Padarn Railway run through it and part of it is still used by the Llanberis Lake Railway. Behind the workshops is a row of four Victorian terraced workers' cottages. Originally built at Tanygrisiau near Blaenau Ffestiniog, they were deserted ruins facing demolition when they were rescued, dismantled and painstakingly rebuilt at the museum. They are now decorated and furnished to cover the various periods of occupation. One is from 1861, sparsely furnished but with a cast iron range to provide heat and cooking. Another is from 1900, the period of one the longest lock-outs of industrial Britain, and the third is from 1969, at the very end of the decline of the quarry.

THE BASICS

Distance: 3 miles / 4.8km

Gradient: Mostly flat. Slight gradient and steps up to the Quarry Hospital

Severity: Easy

Approx. time to walk: 2½ hours

Stiles: None

Map: OS Explorer OL17 (Snowdon, Conwy Valley)

Path description: Pavements and surfaced footpaths

Start point: Car park next to the Electric Mountain visitor centre, Llanberis (GR SH 580601)

Parking: Car park (charge) next to the Electric Mountain Visitor Centre in Llanberis (LL55 4UR)

Dog friendly: Good dog walk

Public toilets: In visitor centre

Nearest food: In visitor centre and there is a café opposite the car park

1. Leave the car park via a metal gate on the left-hand side. Walk along the pavement, passing the Electric Mountain Visitor Centre, then turn left following signs for the Welsh Slate Museum, Castell Dolbadarn and Padarn Country Park. Walk along this road for a short distance then turn right to visit the castle. Then return to the road and continue to its end and turn left.

2. Walk along here, going through a metal gate. Follow the road as it curves right past the Slate Museum. Turn left and bear left through the car park here, passing the toilets and craft workshops, then turn right behind them and follow a road round the car park and turn left onto a footpath towards the Quarry Hospital and Padarn Lake Walk.

3. Head uphill then turn left where the path forks. Follow red, green, yellow and white way-markers to arrive at a viewing area with grand views across the lake. Then climb several sets of steps to reach the Quarry Hospital Museum. After visiting it turn left and continue along the path, through the gateposts of the hospital grounds and downhill on a lane following red, yellow and blue way-markers. Go under a bridge, then stop to have a good look at the scar in the hillside that is the Vivian Quarry. Just before a second bridge turn right at a yellow green and blue way-marker to go between two stone walls then almost immediately turn right and go downhill along the side of an inclined railway. Veer left through the

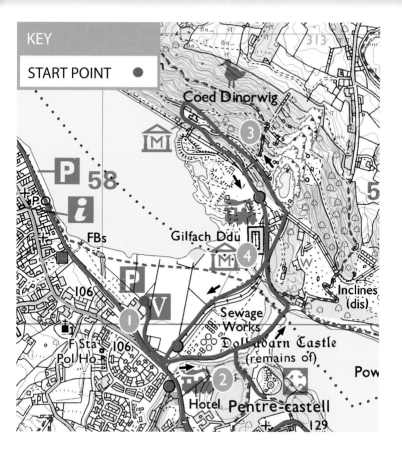

station and cross the tracks, then the road and turn left to visit the Slate Museum. This is totally free and is superb.

4. When you have finished your visit pass the museum, heading back on your outward journey. At the end of the museum perimeter wall turn right, cross a footbridge, go through a gate and continue along a track. This passes Llanberis Station on the Llanberis Lake Railway. Go through a gate, pass the station, follow the path round to the right then exit via a gate onto the road. Turn right and continue back to the car park.

BEDDGELERT

A LEGENDARY DOG, RUPERT THE BEAR AND A HERITAGE
RAILWAY ARE ALL ASSOCIATED WITH THIS GEM OF A WALK.

You may notice the brand name Gelert on some of your outdoor kit. This is where the company was formed in 1975, taking its name from the legendary hound of Prince Llywelyn the Great. It moved its headquarters to nearby Porthmadog in 2003 but retained a shop here.

The famous cartoon bear, Rupert, has a strong connection with this village. In 1956, Alfred Bestall, who produced the superb illustrations in the Rupert Bear Annual, bought a cottage in Beddgelert after having holidayed here for many years. Unsurprisingly he drew inspiration for the annual covers from the landscape around here and continued producing them until 1973.

You will have several encounters with the Welsh Highland Railway as part of its 25 miles of track run through this area and the station near the start of the walk is part of it. It starts in Caernarfon and runs to Porthmadog where it connects to the Ffestiniog Railway and the Welsh Highland Heritage Railway.

Towards the end of this walk you will come across the grave of Gelert, a statue of the dog and a plaque that tells you the story. Way back in the mists of history, in the 13th century, Welsh Prince Llywelyn the Great had a dog called Gelert. One day Llywelyn went hunting without his dog. When he returned the dog greeted him, but Llywelyn noticed that it was covered with blood. This alarmed him and he went into the room where his infant son had been sleeping. The cot was empty and his son's blood-stained clothes lay scattered on the floor. He assumed that Gelert had killed him and in grief he ran his sword through the dog's side, killing it. The dog yelled as it was dying, and this was answered by the cry of a child. Llywelyn then found his son lying nearby, unharmed, but beside him the body of a huge wolf.

It had attacked the boy and Gelert had fought it off and killed it. Full or remorse for having slain his dog, Llywelyn buried his faithful hound and thereafter the place became known as Beddgelert: Gelert's grave.

Some say that the gravesite was created by a landlord of the Goat Hotel in the 18th century to drum up business. We prefer to believe the story.

THE BASICS

Distance: 2¾ miles / 4.4km
Gradient: Very slight gradients
Severity: Easy
Approx. time to walk: 1¾ hours
Stiles: None
Map: OS Explorer OL17 (Snowdon, Conwy Valley)
Path description: Lanes, roads and footpaths
Start point: Car park in Beddgelert (GR SH 588481)
Parking: Car Park in Beddgelert village (charge) (LL55 4YJ)
Dog friendly: Perfect for dogs
Public toilets: Near the bridge in the village towards the end of the walk
Nearest food: Several tearooms, cafes and hotels in the village

BEDDGELERT WALK

1. Exit the car park through a gate in the far left-hand corner from the entrance. There's a finger post pointing to Rhyd Ddu 7.6km (4.8 miles). Head up this path then turn right onto a lane that goes past the steps up to the Welsh Highland Railway Station. The lane becomes a track, goes through a gate then under a railway bridge before turning right again. Then go through a gate on your left and turn right onto a marked footpath. This is a short section that follows the stream and then crosses a bridge to re-join the lane.

2. Turn left and keep on the road to cross the railway. Then the lane becomes a track and once again crosses the railway. When you reach a finger post pointing right to Rhyd Ddu, keep ahead. Then as you approach a metal gate turn left and pass to the right of a house. Keep on this track as it passes another house then turns left in front of a third before bearing right along another track between two fences. Keep walking until you reach a metal gate on your left.

3. Go through this and head downhill and through woodland to go through another gate and arrive beside the railway once more. Turn right and follow the grassy track along the side of the railway. Keep going to pass a barn on your left then cross a bridge and turn right onto a lane.

4. Follow this downhill then just before a railway bridge, then turn right onto a track signposted to Beddgelert. When you reach the gate on the right that you went through on your outward journey at (1) go through it again but this time turn left. Follow the footpath along past the station then veer left downhill and go through a kissing gate, over a bridge and down some steps to cross a lane and continue downhill on a footpath. When you reach a finger post turn right, then left onto a road and downhill to the Royal Goat Hotel.

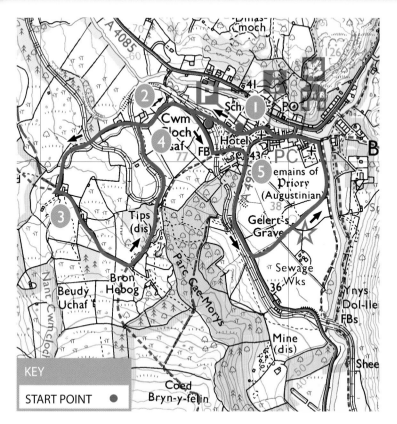

5. Turn right here and proceed with caution along a short section of this road. Go under a railway bridge then turn right and go through a gate and along a track. Follow this until it comes to a gate. Turn left through it to visit the walled compound with a statue of the dog Gelert. This is very popular with children, who love to sit on its back. Follow the path from this compound towards a tree and visit the

actual grave of the dog. Then continue along the path to reach the riverside, turn left and follow the riverside path to go through a metal gate by a metal bridge made in the Glaslyn Foundry in 1951. Turn left here, passing the toilets and some cafés. Then turn left when you reach the street and walk along it to return to the car park.

THE VERY TITLE 'THE PRECIPICE WALK' MAY CONJURE UP IMAGES OF YOU AND YOUR CHILDREN HANGING ON TO A SHEER CLIFF FACE WITH BROKEN FINGERNAILS, BUT NOTHING COULD BE FURTHER FROM THE TRUTH. THERE'S NOT EVEN MUCH OF A CLIMB INVOLVED AND ONCE UP TO THE 800-FOOT LEVEL IT'S SIMPLY A CASE OF FOLLOWING THE NARROW PATH ROUND THE CONTOUR LINE.

There are admittedly a couple of sections where anyone suffering from vertigo might suffer a little, but apart from keeping a close eye on children this really is a superb walk for all the family. And the views are spectacular, particularly along the edge of the Mawddach Valley. Cadair Idris is away to the south. Looking north you should be able to see Snowdon and Moelwynion and over to the west are the Rhinogydd mountains.

The path allegedly follows the line of an ancient Roman watercourse. It certainly utilizes the remains of a tramway that used to be connected to the Voel gold mine. At the very start of the walk you will head uphill through a conifer plantation then via a track and past a house to reach Lake Precipice. You have to be aware that this path is not a right of way and you are only able to enjoy this walk courtesy of an agreement between the Snowdonia National Park Authority and the Nannau Estate. To avoid this becoming a legal right the estate closes the walk each year on 1 February.

The origins of the estate stretch back to sometime in the 11th century, when there is a record of a house being built here. It belonged to a cousin of Owain Glyndŵr. But he supported the English rule and during the Welsh revolt, in the early 15th century, Glyndŵr slew him and destroyed the house. In total five houses have stood on this spot, the last one built in the late 18th century. After the last of the Vaughan family, who owned it, died without an heir in 1956, the house was sold and has had several owners. The house, which you can see on the east side of the lake, is Grade II listed but has unfortunately fallen into a state of disrepair. In January 2015 the owners were served with a notice requiring them to remove a lorry and rotting caravans and tidy the grounds round about.

THE BASICS

Distance: 3½ miles / 5.6km

Gradient: A couple of short but steep climbs

Severity: Moderate

Approx. time to walk: 2 hours

Stiles: None

Map: OS Explorer OL18 (Harlech, Porthmadog and Bala)

Path description: Road, tracks and footpaths, some a bit rocky and uneven

Start point: Llwybr Cynwch Precipice Walk Car Park (GR SH 745211)

Parking: Llwybr Cynwch Precipice Walk Car Park (free), on minor road two miles north of Dolgellau (Nearest postcode is LL40 2NG)

Dog friendly: Yes, very

Public toilets: At car park

Nearest food: Dolgellau

LLANFACHRETH WALK

1. From the car park head towards the road. Just before the exit turn left onto a footpath and follow it to the road. Then take the next turn left, onto a track, beside a footpath finger post. Follow this well-surfaced track uphill then turn right and follow it along the side of a wood. Just before it reaches a stone cottage turn left onto a footpath that runs along the back fence of the garden.

2. The footpath then turns right along the side of a wall. Keep on it as it bends left and continues uphill to reach a gate. Go through this and keep along it with a wall on your right. Soon the lake will come into view. Then go right where the footpath forks and head uphill towards the corner of the wall.

3. Then turn right onto a rougher footpath that now climbs up the hillside and through a gap where a gate used to be. Continue along a narrow footpath that follows the contours of the hill. Take time to enjoy this section and the panoramic views over to your right. Soon the path starts to climb again and becomes much more rocky until it goes through a gap in another wall and continues along a broad grassy path. At a junction keep left following the finger post pointing to the Precipice Walk.

4. It's impossible to get lost on this next section. Just keep following the path. It's narrow and at times rather rocky and there are sections where you will be close to the edge, so keep a hold on young children. But the views along the valley are awesome. Go through a gate, and continue on the path until it starts to curve left towards a gate in a wall. Turn right here and in a short distance you will come to a viewpoint with a memorial bench. It's a great spot for a picnic and the views along the valley from it are fantastic.

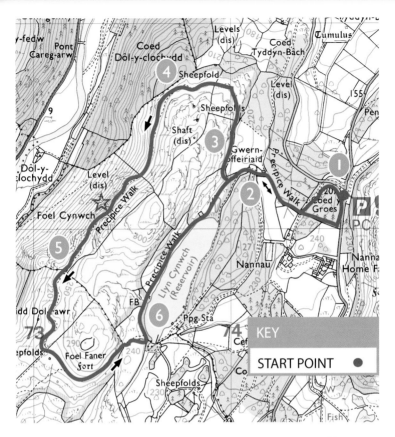

5. Retrace your steps to the path and head on through the gate. Keep following this path until you reach the end of the lake. Then turn left at a finger post marked Precipice Walk.

6. Continue along the edge of the lake on a well-made path then continue beyond the lake to arrive back at point 3. Retrace your outward route from here until you come to a fork in the track heading back to the road. Turn right here onto a footpath, which runs downhill behind the toilets to emerge at the far end of the car park.

NANT GWRTHEYRN

A WELSH LANGUAGE CENTRE, A BUNCH OF HIPPIES AND A VANISHED INDUSTRIAL COMMUNITY ARE THE MAIN ATTRACTIONS ON THIS WALK. OH, AND, OF COURSE, THE SCENERY.

As you head downhill the first thing you will notice is the abandoned quarry and below it the ruins of a farmstead. Fairly recently if you had continued on to Nant Gwrtheyrn you would have encountered a ruined village, windowless and roofless buildings and everywhere overgrown. Today it is a magnificently restored centre for furthering the Welsh language.

The mid-19th century saw the start of an industry in this area that would eventually build a community. Rapidly expanding cities needed granite setts for cobbled streets and a quarry was opened nearby to meet that demand. Eventually three quarries operated here. Accommodation was built for the workers and that was the start of the village. By 1900 it was well established with a population of over 200. It had a cooperative shop, where workers had accounts, which they settled every second Saturday when they were paid. The large house at the end of the village was the quarry manager's house. Eileen M. Webb, daughter of the quarry manager, wrote a book about life here in the 1930s, called This Valley Was Ours, which was published in 1983.

Unfortunately, tarmac replaced cobbles and as the demand for granite decreased there were closures and lay-offs in the quarries. Many people moved away for work. There was a brief revival in the 1930s but the outbreak of World War II signalled the end. Some homeless families squatted in the empty houses, which led to the re-opening of the school, and the community limped on for a few years more.

In the 1970s a group of hippies formed the New Atlantic Community here. They had no electricity or running water or sewerage and wreaked havoc as they tore the place apart. Doors and floorboards were burned for fuel and the roofs were stripped. When the hippies finally moved on, the place was a ruin. Its transformation from derelict village to language centre came about as a result of an Englishman arriving to take over as the only doctor in Llanaelhaearn.

Dr Carl Clowes wanted his kids to grow up speaking Welsh and along with others was involved in creating the trust that would eventually buy and re-build Nant Gwrtheyrn. The first Welsh language course was held here in 1982.

THE BASICS

Distance: 3½ miles / 5.6km

Gradient: A long slow walk downhill to the village and an even slower walk back up the coastal path

Severity: Severe

Approx time to walk: 2½ - 3 hours

Stiles: One

Maps: OS Explorer 253 (Lleyn Peninsula West)

Path description: Well-surfaced lane, coastal footpath and grassy fields

Start Point: Car park above the village (GR SH 353440)

Parking: Car park on minor road off B4417 north of Llithfaen (LL53 6NU)

Dog friendly: Not dog friendly

Public toilets: At village on the walk

Nearest food: Café in the village

NANT GWRTHEYRN WALK

1. Exit the car park and head downhill on the road to Nant Gwtheryn. This descends all the way, going round some corkscrew turns, but has excellent views of the old mine workings on the hills to your right. When you reach the village take some time to explore it and read the interpretation boards. You will pass the Heritage Centre, toilets for walkers (with a pay phone inside) and the café. Then continue downhill on the coastal path, past some picnic tables.

2. Go through a gate and downhill towards the beach and some old quarry buildings. These are in a dangerous condition so keep well away.

3. The path now heads away from the beach and this is the start of the long climb back uphill. The first section is relatively short and then it eases, following the contour of the hill. There are steps on the steepest bits just to make life easier and a rather unusual wooden bench where you can rest for a while and admire the views. Eventually you will arrive at the point where you need to leave the coastal path at Ciliau Isaf.

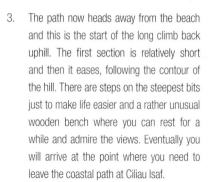

4. Climb up some steps and through a gate. Then skirt past the house on the access track, which then turns right and left. Keep on this and look out for a footpath sign pointing uphill to the left.

5. Head up here over a stile and follow the fence to the top. Then go through a gate in the wall on your left. Turn left to go past a way-marker post, then left though another gate. Follow the path along the fence here and keep on it as it veers slightly right, over

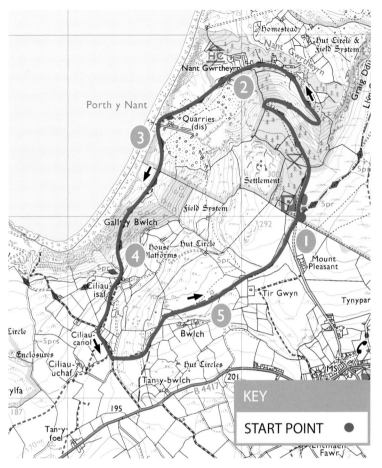

KEY

START POINT ●

the brow of the hill and through another gate. Then continue ahead over the grassy field towards another gate. Go through this and head to the left of the white cottage of Tir Gwyn.

6. A distinct path goes through a gap in the fence at the cottage then veers left to cross another field. When you reach the corner of this go through a gate and on across some heather moorland towards a finger post. Then turn left and re-enter the car park.

PISTYLL

A WALK ALONG THE COASTAL PATH IN SEARCH OF A
FICTIONAL FRENCH DETECTIVE.

The small pilgrims' church at the start of the walk is dedicated to St Beuno, a holy man who lived in the 7th century and was associated with the Llyn Peninsula. There has been a church on this site since medieval times. The font dates back to the 11th century but the building is mostly 15th century. It has a five-bay arch-braced roof, which was still thatched well into the 20th century. One of the delights of visiting this church is finding the floor strewn with rushes and wild flowers and bunches of fragrant herbs fastened to the pews. Outside is what remains of a fishpond and later you will pass what is left of the holy well, which supplied the early church.

In the churchyard seek out the grave of Rupert Davies. Those of a certain age will remember him in the role of Georges Simenon's quintessentially Parisian detective, Maigret. The English version ran for four seasons from 1960 and was memorable for its opening sequence, where a match got struck against a wall, illuminating Maigret's face as he lit his pipe. Ron Grainer's theme in the style of a Parisian street accordion rounded it off. Davies, an Englishman, apparently loved this part of Wales and spent many holidays here.

Much of the first part of this walk is along the Wales Coastal Path and is well served with the distinctive blue way-markers. Thereafter there is a lengthy section along the main road through the hamlet of Pisyyll. Stop at the abandoned Capel Bethania on the side of the road to find the plaque on the wall dedicated to the Calvinistic Methodist Minister, Tom Nefyn Williams. He started his working life in the granite quarries but enlisted in the army in 1914 and fought in the Dardanelles, France and Palestine, where he was wounded. His war experiences made him a life-long pacifist. On his return he studied for the ministry and was ordained in 1925. He soon fell foul of the church, because of some of his doctrinal views and his socialism, reflected in sermons on wages and poor housing.

In 1928 he was ejected from his church. Eventually he returned but remained a controversial preacher until his death in 1958. He was buried at the Church at Edern where he was the minister.

THE BASICS

Distance: 2 miles / 3.2km

Gradient: A few slight gradients

Severity: Easy

Approx. time to walk: 1 hour

Stiles: Two

Map: OS Explorer 253 (Lleyn Peninsula West)

Path description: Footpaths and roads

Start point: St Beuno's Church (GR SH 327420)

Parking: At St Beuno's Church on the B4417 to the east of Pistyll. Limited numbers so please don't park there during a service (LL53 6LR)

Dog friendly: No

Public toilets: None; nearest at Nefyn

Nearest food: Nefyn

PISTYLL WALK

1. From the church head along the track past the fishpond. Then turn left before the drive to some cottages and go through a gate onto the coastal path. Keep ahead along a wall to go through a gate then continue walking beside the wall to climb another wall in front of you via a stile. Then go through a gate, cross a lane, go through another gate then veer right onto a clear path. Go through a metal kissing gate and follow the path as it veers right then go through another metal kissing age and follow the path along the side of a field. When the fence ends veer left, uphill to the far end of a ruined building. Pass this and then turn left over a stile and follow the edge of the next field to reach a metal kissing gate in the far corner. Go through that and a single metal gate beyond then turn left onto the road.

2. Follow the road through the hamlet of Pistyll, passing the tumbledown Capel Bethania Chapel on your left. At the next junction turn left then go right through a kissing gate onto National Trust land.

3. Follow the path uphill and to the left. Look for a signpost marking the spot of the holy well that once served the church. Continue to rise on this path then go through another kissing gate and turn left. Here is the best vantage point for a photograph of the church. Head downhill from here on a faint path following the line of the fence. At the bottom go through a gate then turn immediately left through a kissing gate and walk along a track that is part of the coastal path to reach the entrance to the churchyard on your right.

4. Turn right immediately on entering and walk along the back wall to the highest point. That's where you'll find the gravestone of Rupert Davies, the actor who was famous for playing the French detective Maigret. He is buried here along with his wife. After walking round the churchyard explore inside the building itself then return to the gate. Turn right onto the path and return to the start.

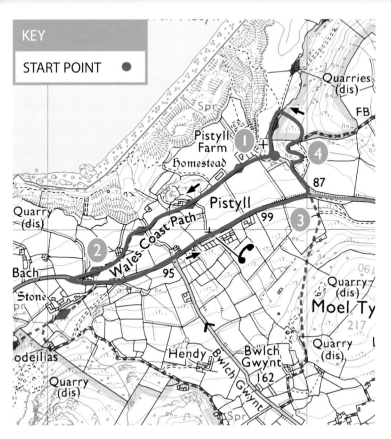

KEY

START POINT ●

LLANYSTUMDWY

A PLEASANT STROLL AROUND THE COUNTRYSIDE THAT
WAS THE BOYHOOD HOME OF ONE OF BRITAIN'S MOST
CHARISMATIC PRIME MINISTERS.

David Lloyd George was born in England but his parents were Welsh and they returned to Wales when he was but a few months old. He was plain David George in these days. The Lloyd he added later in honour of his uncle, with whom he and his mother lived after the death of his father. One of the first buildings you pass on this walk is the house of Richard Lloyd, village shoemaker, a minster and a staunch Liberal. Uncle Richard was a considerable influence on the boy, giving him books and pamphlets to study and encouraging him to take up a career in law and ultimately in politics. He lived long enough to see his protégé become prime minister.

The story of Lloyd George's life is well covered in the museum. He was articled as a solicitor in Porthmadog but as soon as he qualified he opened his own practice in a room at his uncle's. He did very well, took his brother into partnership and opened other offices in neighbouring towns. He was involved politically, campaigning for the Liberal Party. He entered local government as an alderman for Carnarvonshire County Council in 1889. The following year he was elected as the local MP and remained at Westminster for 55 years. By 1906 he was promoted to the Cabinet and from 1908 to 1915 was Chancellor of the Exchequer. When he became prime minister of the wartime coalition in 1916 he set many records that have never been broken. He was the only Welshman and solicitor to have held that office. He was also the last Liberal to do so. He was prime minister until October 1922, when a variety of scandals including the awarding of honours for money brought about his downfall.

However, he remained as a Member of Parliament until 1944 and became a peer in January 1945, but he did not live to take up his seat in the Lords.

He was already in poor health from the cancer that eventually killed him and had returned to live in Llanystumdwy. You will pass his house, Tŷ Newydd, which is now the National Writing Centre for Wales. He died there at the age of 82 on 26 March 1945 and was buried beside the River Dwyfor.

THE BASICS

Distance: 3¼ miles / 5.2km

Gradient: A couple of short very easy gradients, otherwise flat

Severity: Easy

Approx. time to walk: 2 hours

Stiles: Three

Map: OS Explorer 254 (Lleyn Peninsula East)

Path description: Road, pavement, tracks and footpaths

Start point: Car park in Llanystumdwy (GR SH 476383)

Parking: Car park in centre of Llanystumdwy (free), off A497 just west of Criccieth (LL52 0SG)

Dog friendly: No really. Stiles could be a problem and they must be kept on a short lead for much of the walk

Public toilets: On the main street just past the museum

Nearest food: The Feathers, along from the car park, or in Pwllheli

LLANYSTUMDWY WALK

1. Turn right out of the car park and head along the street passing The Feathers on your left, Lloyd George's childhood home on the right and arriving at the museum. You can leave this until after the walk if you have time. It has a splendid video, which takes 20 minutes and is well worth viewing.

2. Continue along the street past the toilets then cross the road and turn left along a public footpath. Walk along this lane and keep going when it reduces to a narrow footpath. Go through a gate at the end and very carefully cross the road.

3. On the other side follow a footpath sign along the drive to Aberkin. Keep on this road as it bends left to go past a farm steading then to the right of the farmhouse, where it bends left again. Go across a stile to the right of a gate then go left across to another gate and go through a gate beside that. Turn left to re-gain the track and walk along it to reach another stile just before a railway line. Cross this with care and go across another stile beyond it. Then continue

along the track, which will turn left to follow a field boundary and eventually reach a kissing gate.

4. Go through this and onto the coastal path. Follow this until you come to some black huts then turn right onto another track.

5. Keep on this track, ignoring junctions until you reach a bridge over the railway. Cross this and keep on the track, which becomes a lane, to reach the road. Again cross with care and go through a kissing gate on the other side.

6. Follow this narrow grassy path uphill to reach a short wall beside a garden gate. Climb the steps over this wall and keep left along the path. Then go through a

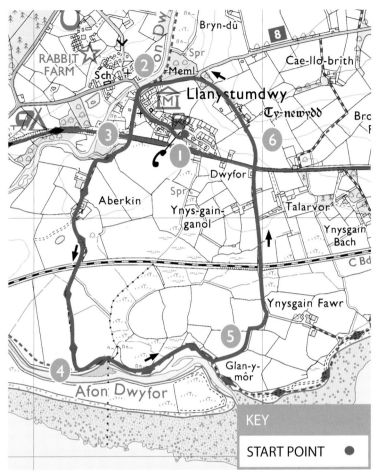

KEY

START POINT ●

kissing gate, turn left to pass a cottage, veer left across a car park area and out onto the drive in front of Ty Newydd National Writers' Centre for Wales. Follow the drive down to meet the main road then turn left. Continue down this road towards the village, passing the memorial at Lloyd George's grave on the right. When you reach a T-junction turn left and walk along the street to return to the car park.

RHYD

ANCIENT OAK WOODS, AN ARTIFICIAL LAKE AND A CLASSIC
RAILWAY ARE ALL ENCOUNTERED ON THIS DELIGHTFUL WALK
THROUGH WHAT WAS ONCE THE TAN-Y-BWLCH ESTATE.

Mary's Lake (Llyn Mair) was apparently created as a 21st birthday present for Mary, the daughter of landowner William Oakley. His home, Plas Tan-y-bwlch, was reputed to be the first house in Wales to have hydroelectric power, which was generated by a Pelton wheel that was fed with water from the Llyn Mair. The house is now the Snowdownia National Park Environmental Studies Centre.

The Oakley family derived most of their wealth from slate quarries and owned the largest underground slate mine in the world at Blaenau Ffestiniog. It operated under different owners until it finally closed in 2010. The slate was transported from the quarries to Porthmadog on the narrow-gauge Ffestiniog Railway, which runs through the estate. It started operating in 1836. It was built so that it was effectively running downhill all the way to Porthmadog. To create the incline the engineers built the tracks so that they followed the contours of the landscape and constructed embankments and cuttings. While you are on the walk you will continually hear the engines as they chug uphill, never really being able to identify where they are. Just when you

think they are coming towards you they will change direction and the sound will move away again. The trains ran down using the force of gravity, then horses that travelled in special wagons were used to drag the empty ones back uphill. By 1863 production had outstripped the capacity of the railway and so special steam locomotives were ordered.

A couple of years later the railway started carrying passengers. The railway began to decline from the 1930s and finally ceased to operate in 1946. Fortunately the rails were not lifted, which made restoration easier when a group of enthusiasts acquired it in 1954 and a limited passenger service commenced the next year.

While you meet the railway line at various points on the walk the best chance of seeing the trains is at Tan-y-bwlch station. Tan-y-bwlch was famous for stationmaster Will Jones and his wife Bessie. From 1929 Bessie would greet the passengers off the trains wearing traditional Welsh costume and then serve teas in the station house. She continued to do this when the line re-opened until they retired in 1968.

THE BASICS

Distance: 2½ miles / 4km

Gradient: Some flat bits, a few energetic inclines and some gentle downhill sections

Severity: Easy to moderate

Approx. time to walk: 1½ - 2 hours

Stiles: Two

Map: OS Explorer OL18 (Harlech, Porthmadog and Bala)

Path description: Footpaths, forest tracks and railways

Start point: Car Park at Llyn Mair (GR SH 652413)

Parking: Car park (free) at Llyn Mair on B4410 near Tan-y-Bwlch Station (Nearest postcode LL41 3AQ)

Dog friendly: Yes if they can manage stiles

Public toilets: At Tan-y-Bwlch Station

Nearest food: At station or at the Oakley Arms Hotel at the junction of the A487 and the B4410 about a mile from the start

RHYD WALK

1. Cross the road from the car park and go through a wooden gate then continue along a well-surfaced footpath which runs anti-clockwise round Llyn Mair. When you reach a junction with a way-marker post bearing the number 11, turn right onto the Wales Coast Path.

2. You now head away from the lake. Keep on this path until you reach a massive beech tree with two trunks. It's easy to spot because it's huge and most of the other trees are birch. Turn right here and head uphill on a few steps then proceed to climb on a footpath through the woods.

3. When you reach the Ffestiniog Railway go over a stile, carefully cross the track, then head up some steps and through a gate at the top then turn right onto a grassy footpath that climbs gently up to the side of a cottage. Turn right here and go through a small car parking area then left onto a forest track. As this approaches another dwelling there is a crossroad of tracks. Turn left and keep going until you reach another junction just by way-marker number 6.

4. Turn right and bear left at the next junction. You will catch glimpses of the railway line below you on your left and hear the train whistle from time to time. Keep on this track ignoring all junctions as you skirt round Llyn Hafod-y-Llyn. Then go past a barrier and turn right onto the road.

5. In just 50 feet turn left onto another road and follow it until it curves to the left. Look out for a footpath sign on your right then climb a stile and onto a woodland footpath. Follow this to reach the station, where you can go straight onto the bridge over the railway and down onto the platform. Spend some time reading the interpretation boards and if you have timed it right watching one of the trains coming in pulling a long line of carriages. You can get something to eat here in the café, use the toilet and find out more about Welsh heritage railways.

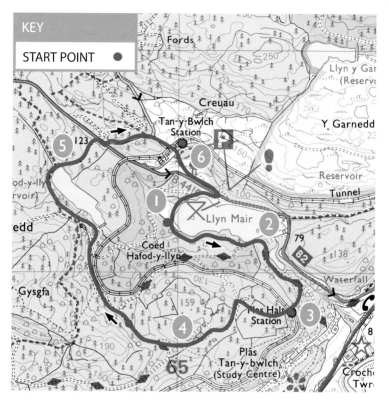

6. Leave the station following a finger post sign to the Nature Trail/ Llyn Mair, head downhill on some steps, keep on the footpath and eventually cross the wooden footbridge back into the car park.

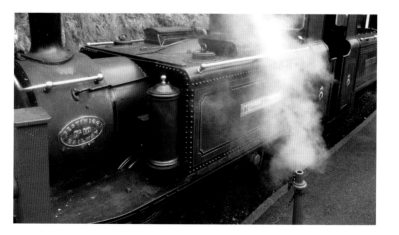

LLANDECWYN

WATERLILIES, DRAGONFLIES, WILDFLOWERS, TWO LAKES AND
A GRUESOME LEGEND ARE ALL ENCOUNTERED ON THIS WALK.

Llyn Tecwyn Isaf is the small lake at the start of this walk. Isaf in Welsh means lower. This is the only place in North Wales where you will fine downy emerald dragonflies. Look out also for hairy dragonflies, keeled skimmers and the small red damselfly.

The other lake is Llyn Tecwyn Uchaf, the upper lake. A dam was built across it in 1896 so that the lake would provide a water supply for Penrhyndeudraeth, Ffestiniog and Porthmadog. A further dam was constructed in 1920 to increase the capacity of the reservoir.

Once you have passed the upper lake, on the return leg you will have superb views across the Afon Dwyryd estuary and the Llyn Peninsula. The fortification in the distance is Harlech Castle. The track downhill from here was once the main county road and may date back as far as the Neolithic. It's now part of the Ardudwy Way, which is 24 miles (40km) long and split into three sections.

It passes an ancient churchyard with a 17th-century stone lychgate that is leaning almost as much as the tower in Pisa and looks in danger of collapse. Don't worry – it's quite safe. The current St Tecwyn's Church is late 19th century but possibly incorporated parts of the earlier medieval building including an 11th-century stone with an inscription. Tecwyn was a 6th-century holy man who allegedly arrived here from Brittany, founding this church and the nearby settlement at Llandecwyn. Regrettably it is not open for visitors.

One local legend associated with this area is attached to the 17th-century grave of a woman called Dorti Lwyd. She was an old woman, living on her own, with just a black cat for company. A number of unexplained deaths amongst local cattle led people to accuse her of being a witch. Her fate was a most cruel one. She was placed in a barrel, the lid was sealed and then long nails were driven through the sides.

Her neighbours then threw the barrel from high ground above Llyn Tecwyn. She was apparently buried where the cask stopped, and the spot is marked by a mound of white stones. We never found it. Legend has it that anyone who visits it without adding a stone to the cairn will die within a year.

THE BASICS

Distance: 2½ miles / 4km

Gradient: Mostly long slow, gentle inclines but a couple of very short, steeper ones

Severity: Moderate

Approx. time to walk: 1½ hours

Stiles: Two

Map: OS Explorer OL18 (Harlech, Porthmadog and Bala)

Path description: Lanes, tracks and footpaths

Start point: Lay-by on north side of Llyn Tecwyn Isaf (GR SH 629371)

Parking: Lay-by at Llyn Tecwyn Isaf, on minor road just north of Bryn Bwbach to the east of the A496 south of Penrhyndeudraeth (Nearest postcode LL47 6YS)

Dog friendly: No

Public toilets: Nearest is in Talsarnau

Nearest food: Ship Aground pub in Talsarnau

LLANDECWYN WALK

1. Walk away from the lake in the direction you travelled to get there. Turn right at the fork then go left uphill, through the woods, at a footpath sign. Pass the remains of a gate and continue along the fence line over boggy ground. Then follow the narrow footpath through the woods until it starts going downhill to cross a low stile in the wall, followed by some steps. Continue following the well-marked path through heather and bracken to reach a gate and beyond it a lane.

2. Bear left onto the lane and continue along it, rising steadily for approximately ¾ mile/1.2km passing the drives to Aberdeunant and Perthi on your right. Shortly after passing a stone barn on the left you will see a cottage about a hundred yards or so further on.

3. Turn left just before you reach it onto a faint footpath then go through a gate at the left-hand rear side of the cottage. Follow the direction arrow of the footpath sign and veer right uphill through the garden then exit through a kissing gate and continue along a footpath. This climbs steadily following a wall. When that turns right keep ahead. There should now be a wall on your left. As the path starts to turn right away from the wall veer left onto a faint footpath that heads uphill alongside the wall through rather thick bracken to arrive near a ladder stile.

4. Go through a gap in the wall just to the left of this and follow the wall on your left down towards the water. When you reach a ladder stile on your left, cross it and proceed along the edge of the lake on a narrow footpath through the heather. Note that this can be rather heavy going in the height of summer. Then the path continues through thick bracken before dropping down to a small but lovely shingle beach. Follow this round the lake then head uphill on some rocks to get to the wall across the dam. Cross this exit through a metal gate and turn left onto a track.

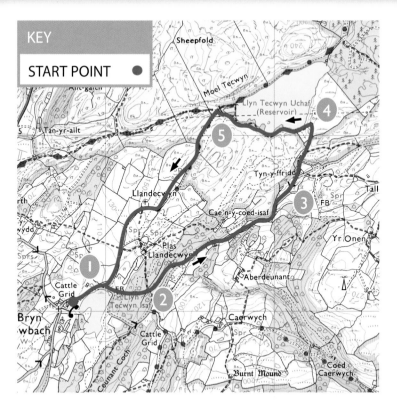

KEY

START POINT ●

5. Walk along this, go through a second gate then take the left-hand track that heads uphill beside a wall. As you reach the top of the hill you will have a great view over the Dwyryd Estuary, over to Portmeirion on your right and ahead of you, slightly to the right, you will see the outline of Harlech Castle. Continue following the track to reach the church at Llandecwyn. Unfortunately this is one that is more often than not closed. From here follow the lane down to the car park.

TAL-Y-BONT

A LOVELY TRANQUIL WALK THROUGH WOODLAND, ALONG THE BANKS OF A RIVER THEN FOLLOWING THE ROUTE OF LONG-FORGOTTEN CATTLE DROVERS PAST PREHISTORIC SETTLEMENTS AND AN ELIZABETHAN MANOR.

This small and sleepy village is a great favourite of Nigel Mansell, former world champion Formula 1 racing driver, who has a home nearby. You soon pass the Ysgethin Inn, which was previously a fulling mill and still has the Pelton wheel which once captured the force of the river to drive the mill. As you go through the woodland along the banks of the Afon Ysgethin, look out for merlin, ring ouzel and jay. You might also be lucky enough to catch sight of a raven or grouse.

The path heads gently uphill until you reach a house called Lletyi Lloegr, which in times long past was an overnight lodging for cattle drovers driving their beasts to the cattle markets of London. From the way-marked sign you will see that this is part of the Ardudwy Way. Just to the right of the house is Pont Fadog, an impressive stone packhorse bridge, built in 1762. The central stone on one side of the bridge has the date and some ornate carving. There's a hole in it about the size of a twopence coin, but its purpose is unknown.

The route from the house now heads left and uphill on a well-surfaced lane and onto moorland. A little further on there is a Neolithic burial chamber. Five millennia ago this was a well-populated area and would have contained various settlements and primitive field systems. At some time in the past, grave robbers uncovered this chamber, removing the protective covering of earth and stones and leaving just an empty tomb.

The last point of historical interest you will pass is Cors-y-Gedol, which literally means The Bog of Hospitality. Now that may seem like a strange name for a fancy house but a few centuries ago this entire area would have been marshland. Although you pass a farm of the same name you will only pass by the gates to the Elizabethan Manor. It was built in 1576 by the Vaughans, a powerful family who had more than a hand in putting Henry Tudor on the throne of England in 1485. They owned it until 1791 when the last of them died without an heir. Nowadays it is a well-used venue for weddings.

THE BASICS

Distance: 2½ miles / 4km

Gradient: Gentle apart from a couple of short climbs

Severity: Moderate

Approx. time to walk: 2 hours

Stiles: None

Map: OS Explorer OL18 (Harlech, Porthmadog and Bala)

Path description: Footpaths, mostly well surfaced, with a few rough sections and country lanes

Start point: Car park in Tal-y-bont (GD SH 589218)

Parking: Car park (free) at Tal-y-Bont, beside the main road A496 (LL43 2AN)

Dog friendly: A good dog walk

Public toilets: At car park

Nearest food: Ysgethin Inn, on the walk very near the start

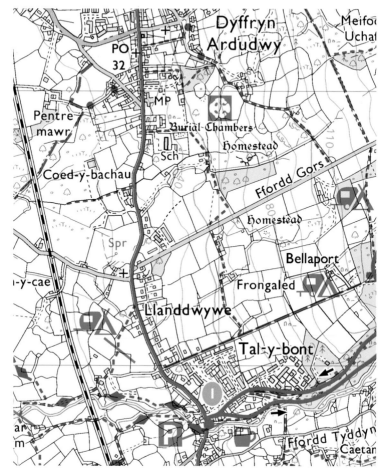

1. Leave the car park on the riverside path and turn left. Continue along this path, passing to the left of the Ysgethin Inn. Then veer slightly right to pass to the right of a small building. Enjoy a pleasant stroll by the river, keeping right at the first path junction, then turn right again after a short climb brings you to a T-junction. As long as the river is to your right you will be fine. Keep right at the next junction, through a gate and keep on to the end of the path in front of a stone cottage.

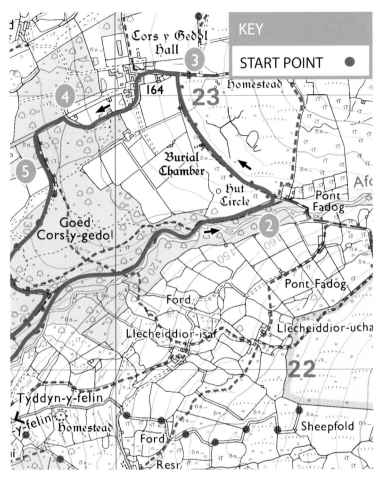

KEY

START POINT ●

Turn right and go downhill a little on a lane to visit the Pont Fadog bridge that was built in 1762. When you have seen it return to the cottage.

2. Then keep ahead on a narrow lane and look out for a small Neolithic burial chamber on the left. Then continue along the lane to reach a gate. Go through it and turn left onto another lane.

3. In a short distance the lane turns left in front

of a drive to a house. Keep to the lane, which will then turn right and left again on the far side of a farm. Keep ahead past some stone farm buildings on the right.

4. The lane turns left again just in front of the entrance to Cors-y-Gedol Hall. You are now heading away from the entrance down a broad, tree-lined road. Look out for a footpath sign on the left-hand side a couple of hundred yards along and turn left to go through a gate and onto a broad footpath.

5. Follow this along the side of a wall. When it narrows keep ahead and eventually reach a gate. Go through this. When the path forks keep right, through woodlands and when it forks again keep right, along the edge of the wood by a fence. When you come to a small footbridge over a stream turn left and follow the path by the stream until it heads downhill to reach a wider path. Turn left onto this and continue ahead. Keep going when it runs into a tarmac lane and ultimately reaches a T-junction with a road.

6. Turn left and head downhill to arrive back at the car park.

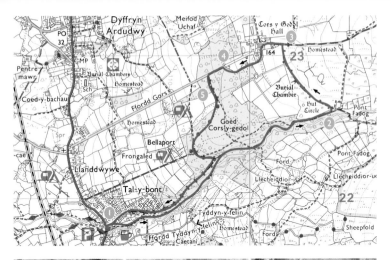

ABOUT THE AUTHOR

Moira McCrossan and Hugh Taylor are a husband and wife writing team now specialising in travel for the over 50's and walking guides. They are also travel editors of the UK's premier over 50's web site laterlife.com.

Moira McCrossan spent most of her working life in education and was a Primary School Head Teacher. An active trade unionist she is a former President of the Educational Institute of Scotland, served on the general council of the Scottish TUC and the executive committee of the Women's National Commission for whom she co-authored the report, Growing up Female in the UK. She was also a frequent contributor to the Times Educational Supplement (Scotland).

Hugh Taylor is an Award winning travel writer, broadcaster and photographer. He worked extensively for BBC Radio, producing several series for Radio 2 including Doomsday in the Afternoon about the music of the Scottish Travellers.

Together they have written or contributed to over forty travel and outdoor guides, some of which have been translated into several languages. They range from major country guides covering Scotland, Lebanon and Jordan to walking books throughout the UK. Their work has appeared worldwide in publications as diverse as The Times, Women's Realm, Choice, The Herald, Interval World and the Glencairn Gazette. They live in the picturesque southern Scottish village of Moniaive and in Capena, a hill town just north of Rome.

The Authors would like to thank the team at the Camping and Caravanning Club Press Office for all their help, Bob and Sylvia Currie for giving us the use of their splendid house on the Menai Straits and Peter Hewlett of Walking North Wales for invaluable advice and for loaning us many books. www.walkingnorthwales.co.uk